HOTSPOTS
MALTA

Written by Paul Murphy, updated by Donna Dailey
Front cover photography courtesy of Thomas Cook Tour Operations Ltd

Original design concept by Studio 183 Limited
Series design by the Bridgewater Book Company
Cover design/artwork by Lee Biggadike, Studio 183 Limited

Produced by the Bridgewater Book Company
The Old Candlemakers, West Street, Lewes, East Sussex BN7 2NZ, United Kingdom
www.bridgewaterbooks.co.uk
Project Editor: Emily Casey Bailey
Project Designer: Lisa McCormick

Published by Thomas Cook Publishing
A division of Thomas Cook Tour Operations Limited
PO Box 227, Units 15-16, Coningsby Road, Peterborough PE3 8SB, United Kingdom
email: books@thomascook.com
www.thomascookpublishing.com
+ 44 (0) 1733 416477

ISBN-13: 978-1-84157-528-5
ISBN-10: 1-84157-528-3

First edition © 2006 Thomas Cook Publishing
Text © 2006 Thomas Cook Publishing
Maps © 2006 Thomas Cook Publishing
Head of Thomas Cook Publishing: Chris Young
Project Editor: Diane Ashmore
Production/DTP Editor: Steven Collins

Printed and bound in Spain by Graficas Cems, Navarra, Spain

CONTENTS

SYMBOLS KEY

The following is a key to the symbols used throughout this book:

i	information office	**police**	police station	**café**	café
bus	bus stop	**tip**	tip	**bar**	bar
post	post office	**shopping**	shopping	**fine**	fine dining
church	church	**restaurant**	restaurant		

---

① telephone   **ⓕ** fax   **ⓔ** email   **ⓦ** website address

ⓐ address   **ⓛ** opening times   **ⓘ** important

€ budget price   **€€** mid-range price   **€€€** most expensive

★ specialist interest   **★★** see if passing   **★★★** top attraction

---

Ramla
Bay

San Blas
Bay

QBAJJAR
MARSALFORN

ZEBBUG

GOZO

Ta' Pinu
Basilica

XAGHRA

GHARB

Ggantija

NADUR

QALA

Azure
Window

**VICTORIA
(RABAT)**

MGARR

XEWKIJA

Blue
Lagoon

COMINO

XLENDI

SANNAT

MEDITERRANEAN SEA

Marfa Ridge

M

**POPEYE
VILLAGE**

Golden Bay

Gh

G
B

EUROPE

SICILY

MALTA

AFRICA

ASIA

MEDITERRANEAN SEA

N

0 1 2 3 4 5 km
0 1 2 3 miles

I's
s
I's
e

QAWRA

BUGIBBA
ST. PAUL'S BAY

PACEVILLE
ST. JULIAN'S

SLIEMA

VALLETTA

VITTORIOSA

SENGLEA

BIEH

MOSTA

TA' QALI

MALTA

PAOLA

Tarxien
Temples

ZEJTUN

MDINA

LUQA

RABAT

• Busket Gardens

253 m

BIRZEBBUGA

Marsaxlokk
Bay

li Cliffs

Hagar
Qim

Blue
Grotto

Getting to know Malta

The Maltese islands form a small Mediterranean archipelago, consisting of Malta, Gozo, Comino, Cominotto and Filfla. Malta is the largest member of the group and is by far the most popular as a holiday destination. Measuring 21 km (13 miles) wide by 14 km (9 miles) deep at its furthest points, and some 27 km (17 miles) from corner to corner, it is similar in size to the Isle of Wight. Gozo is smaller still, measuring 14 km (9 miles) by 6.5 km (4 miles), while Comino is just 1.5 sq km (1 sq mile) in area. Cominotto and Filfla are tiny, uninhabited rocks.

THE PEOPLE

Despite Malta's geography and climate, the Maltese are not hot-blooded Mediterraneans. Far from it – they have a calm, friendly and philosophical approach to life, which most British visitors recognise as being very similar to their own. Perhaps this is not surprising when you consider that the British were an integral part of Maltese life from 1800 to 1979.

The Maltese do have a Latin streak, however. You will see this if you join in with the evening *passegiata* (promenade), or watch a family group shouting and laughing at each other across the tables of the local pizzeria, or, best of all, revelling in the celebrations of the local town or village *festa* (festival).

BRITISH INFLUENCE

The British love affair with Malta goes back a long way. Just over 200 years ago Britain liberated the island from the tyranny of Napoleon. From that date until Maltese Independence in 1964 (and the final departure of the British services in 1979), Britain used the island as a strategic naval base.

During this period, the islanders were bestowed with British icons such as red post boxes, blue police lamps and Watney's Red Barrel beer, as well as British vehicles such as the Ford Prefect, the Austin Seven, the

● *Azure Window, Gozo*

Morris Minor and the British Leyland bus. One of the island's more curious attractions is that many of these symbols of yesteryear are still here today. Visiting Malta is a great trip down memory lane for anyone British, aged 40 and above.

UNDER SIEGE

Although Malta is famous today as a lazy sunshine holiday destination it has been host to two of the most famous and heroic sieges in world history. In fact, it is no exaggeration to say that incredibly not just once – but, twice – events on this tiny rock have shaped the course of world history.

In 1565 the island was the decisive battleground in the conflict between the army of Islam and the forces of Christianity. Surging westwards, the Ottoman Empire had their sights on the European mainland but first they had to eliminate the thorny problem of Malta, home to the Crusader Knights of St John.

The Turks, some 40,000 strong, outnumbered the Knights and Maltese defenders by over four to one, but the Knights were better organised and defended the island magnificently in four months of bloody hand-to-hand fighting. The Knights were down to their last 600 men, and on the point of defeat, when help finally arrived. The Turks meanwhile had lost 30,000 men and retreated, never again to threaten the West.

CRUISING

Spend a wonderful lazy day seeing Malta as travellers did for centuries before the arrival of the aeroplane.
Comino's Blue Lagoon (see page 79) is one of the most beautiful patches of sea in the whole Mediterranean, while **Gozo's Azure Window** is a stupendous natural rock formation (see page 68).

NEIGHBOURS

The nearest land to the Maltese islands is Sicily, 95 km (60 miles) to the north. Tunisia lies 290 km (180 miles) due west – in fact Malta lies further south than the North African capitals of Tunis and Rabat in Morocco.

WORLD WAR II

If the Great Siege of 1565 was stirring stuff, then the Second Great Siege of World War II was to be every bit as relentless and just as important.

Once again, because of its geographical position, Malta assumed huge importance as the focal point of the Mediterranean and North African conflicts. For the Allies, it was a vital base from which to harry the enemy and stop supplies reaching Rommel in North Africa, but at the same time it was isolated and within easy bombing range of Axis-held Sicily.

When Mussolini failed to subdue the island, Hitler brought the full fury of the Luftwaffe to bear. During 1942, Malta endured 154 days and nights of Blitz, which far outweighed even London's suffering. In fact, Malta was recorded as being the most bombed place on earth.

Somehow the islanders dug in and resisted and, although human casualties were relatively low (around 2200 lost their lives), parts of the island were bombed to oblivion. Throughout this, the vital supply convoys continued, and the Allies went on to win the all-important battle for North Africa. As a mark of respect, Britain awarded the island, and by implication every single islander, the George Cross, the highest award for civilian gallantry.

In April 2002 the Princess Royal, Princess Anne, was the guest of honour in the celebrations marking the sixtieth anniversary of the George Cross awarded by her grandfather – George VI.

The best of the Maltese islands

GOZO

Gozo is the Maltese island where time stands still. If you only have a day then an excursion here (see page 67) will probably include the fortified Citadel perched above the capital of Victoria, the spectacular natural rock-and-sea formations at Dwejra and the miraculous Basilica of Ta'Pinu. An even better idea is to spend a couple of nights here in a beautifully converted farmhouse, discovering such treasures as Gharb's village square and folklore museum, and the beach at Ramla Bay.

IN GUARDIA

History has never been so colourful as at this re-enactment of a military parade in Valletta's historic Fort St Elmo (see page 40). There's plenty of shouting, brandishing of weaponry, and flashes and bangs too, so it's great for all the family. 'In Guardia' happens on Sunday, around once every fortnight between September and June. The re-enactments start at 11.00 and last for about 45 minutes. Ask your resort representative for dates and details.

MALTA PANORAMA

Spend a varied day away from the resorts looking at some of Malta's architectural and historic gems, its favourite fishing village, the opportunity for some shopping and a meal at one of the island's leafiest and most pleasant spots. The highlight is the atmospheric ancient town of Mdina, from whose bastions there are views which cover over half the island (see page 56).

SICILY

The highlights of the excursion to this beautiful mountainous island are Mount Etna, Europe's highest and most active volcano, and Taormina, one of the most charming and romantic small towns in the Mediterranean. It's a very long day but most visitors agree it's worthwhile (see page 92).

Sliema
fashionable seafront resort

Sliema (pronounced 'Slee-ma') enjoys two waterfronts – one faces the Mediterranean while the other is formed by Marsamxett Harbour (pronounced 'Mar-sam-shett'). The latter enjoys picture-postcard views across to Valletta, a ferry giving easy access to the capital, and a good selection of eating and drinking places.

Sliema is not only one of Malta's most popular resorts – it is also one of the island's most fashionable residential addresses on account of its seafront setting, its proximity to Valletta, and its shopping, eating and drinking facilities. Stretched across a peninsula, Sliema has no obvious centre, but its heart lies along the stretch known as the **Strand** and **Tigne Seafront**, which faces Valletta. By day, international shops, such as Stefanel and Marks & Spencer, attract local residents, while small independent shops, particularly along Bisazza Street (which cuts through from Tower Road to the Strand), welcome holidaymakers. On a summer night there is barely a seat to be had in the cafés, bars and restaurants that face the seafront promenade.

From the Strand, the night-time views of Valletta, illuminated across the harbour, are among the most magical on the island. At the tip of the headland is **Tigne Fort**, the last of the defences built by the Knights in 1792. Inland from the Strand is Sliema's residential quarter, which is worth exploring on a cool morning stroll for a look at some fine old houses and villas.

Manoel Island, with an old fort, the Royal Yacht Club and a shipyard, sits in the middle of Sliema Creek. Behind it on the opposite shore are the towns of **Ta'xbiex** and **Msida** – Malta's two main yacht marinas – filled with luxury pleasure craft. You will pass these attractive harbours on the road to Valletta.

THINGS TO SEE & DO
Harbour tours ★★
A cruise around Valletta and the Three Cities is an indispensable part of anyone's visit to Malta. Boats depart regularly from the Strand.

BEACHES
Save for a miniscule patch of sand below the Mariner's Pub (see map on page 14), sunbathing and swimming is 'on the rocks' at Sliema. The rocks are smooth and shelve gradually into the sea, running along the north side of the peninsula to St Julian's Tower. The best public swimming areas can be found on the lidos along Qui Si Sana and Tower Road, and there are also private lidos with restaurants and water sports.

RESTAURANTS (see map on page 14)
Barracuda €€ ❶ Excellent Italian restaurant, specializing in fish, occupying a sturdy 18th-century stone house on the edge of Balluta Bay. Book a table with a waterside view. ⓐ 194 Main Street, Balluta Bay ❶ 21 331 817

SHOPPING
On Bisazza Street, pop in to the four-storey **Plaza Shopping Centre**. Here you will find the top international labels all under one roof. Besides clothes, shoes and fashionable beachwear, the Plaza boasts the islands' finest perfumery, a 'cool' curio shop and the ubiquitous McDonald's. Open Mon–Sat 09.00–13.00 and 16.00–19.00.

Ginza Cute swimwear tops the fashions at this small corner boutique. ⓐ St Dominic Street ❶ 21 343 359

Mil Ideas Jewellery, ceramics and stylishly designed household items are among the gifts to be found in this delightful shop. ⓐ Along Tower Road ❶ 21 342 266

Chez Philipe €€ **2** On the border between Sliema and Gzira, this is a quirky eatery run by a Frenchman. The fare is French provincial; not fancy but wholesome and good. ⓐ 181 The Strand ⓣ 21 330 755

Il Galeone €€ **3** Long regarded as one of the best casual restaurants in Sliema, serving very good Italian food at reasonable prices. ⓐ 35 Tigne seafront ⓣ 21 316 420 ⓛ Closed Sun and Mon

Krishna €€ **4** Sliema's best Indian restaurant with nice decor and some unusual offerings, such as almond fish and *palak gosht* (a spinach dish). ⓐ The Strand ⓣ 21 346 291

Marianna's Tex-Mex Restaurant €€ **5** Bright Mexican prints and south-western kitsch adorn this delightful Mexican restaurant, which boasts the best margaritas on the island. ⓐ 132 Tower Road, opposite the promenade ⓣ 21 318 943

Pastamania € **6** A wide range of pasta, pizzas and gnocchi are served at this cheerful restaurant. You can also dine outside on the shady terrace. ⓐ 254–255 Tower Road ⓣ 21 343 433

The Peak Oriental Cuisine €€ **7** Not an easy place to find, but worth it for the view and the cuisine. The house special, Beijing Duck with a pancake condiment is fabulous. ⓐ Eighth floor of the Plaza Commercial Centre ⓣ 21 314 861 ⓛ Closed Mon

Piccolo Padre € **8** Great little pizzeria in the basement of Barracuda (see page 16). Very lively – ideal for all ages. Book a seat with views on to Balluta Bay. ⓐ 195 Main Street, Balluta Bay ⓣ 21 344 875

San Marino € **9** One of the best of the Strand's numerous cafés and *pasticcerias*, ideal for a beer, an ice cream, a snack or a coffee and cake. ⓐ 29 The Strand

🔺 *Promenade, Sliema*

Surfside € 🔟 Though it looks like any other Tower Road beachside kiosk, the pizzas here are delicious and the crowd is usually very lively. Large terrace overlooking the sea. 🅐 Tower Road, opposite New Tower Palace Hotel 🅣 21 345 384

Ta'Kolina €€ ⓫ Rather staid, but very popular place to try Maltese cooking at its best. Excellent service. 🅐 Tower Road 🅣 21 335 106 🕒 Open daily from 17.30

TGI Fridays €€ ⓬ The winning American formula housed in a 19th-century gun battery. 🅐 Il Fortizza, Tower Road (opposite the Preluna Hotel and Towers) 🅣 21 346 898

NIGHTLIFE
Frenchies Nightclub and Disco ⓭ Huge venue set in the rustic atmosphere of an old fortress, with a smaller club, **The Shelter**, tucked away within. ⓐ Crowne Plaza Hotel ⓣ 21 323 228 ⓛ Open Wed–Sun from 21.00

PROMENADING
When the sun goes down local families come out – as they do all over the Mediterranean – for a *passegiata* (promenade), particularly along Tower Road. Stalls selling Maltese snacks and ice creams, and impromptu markets, are set up to catch the passing trade.

St Julian's & Paceville
nightlife capital

The traditional face of St Julian's is Spinola Bay, a charming fishing harbour full of picturesque fishing boats and one of Malta's most photographed places. Behind here lies the modern quarter of Paceville (pronounced 'Parch-ay-ville'), the island's nightlife centre, chock-a-block with restaurants, bars and discos, with music blaring from every direction.

Between Spinola Bay and the Westin-Dragonara is Paceville, quiet and hung-over by day, throbbing by night. Whilst Paceville attracts a largely young and lively crowd, there are quieter and more discerning establishments around its fringes, where you can have a drink and enjoy authentic Maltese cooking.

At the tip of **Dragonara Point** is one of Malta's three casinos. Around the headland is **St George's Bay**, a narrow, sheltered bay with shallow waters and a small sandy beach, though swimmers have to share the water with moored fishing boats. Here, Paceville merges into St Andrew's, a former British military base. A number of upmarket hotels have developed along the north side of St George's Bay.

 For a special treat, visit the top-quality restaurants of the Westin-Dragonara Resort. There is also a good lido here.

LIDOS
Reef Club The best lido in St Julian's, with waterskiing and windsurfing available, plus a small sandy area.

RESTAURANTS (see map opposite)
 Al Convento €€ **❶** Good Italian food. Book a window seat for the views over Spinola Bay. **ⓐ** Main Street **ⓣ** 21 344750

 Avenue € **❷** Busy, good-value family restaurant, serving steaks, fish, burgers, pasta and salads. **ⓐ** Triq Gorg **ⓣ** 21 311753

⌂ *Spinola Bay, St Julian's*

🍴 **Dolce Vita** €€ ❸ A fine restaurant specializing in seafood, and which overlooks the picturesque Spinola Bay. ⓐ 159 Triq San Gorg, St Julian's ☏ 21 337 036 ⏱ Open daily from 18.00

🔷 **L'Ghonella** €€ ❹ An oasis of calm in a sea of frenzy, with first-class Italian cuisine on the peaceful terrace of the old Spinola Palace. ⓐ Off St George's Road ☏ 21 341 027 ⏱ Open evenings

🍴 **Gullivers** € ❺ Simple, friendly no-frills restaurant specializing in Maltese food. ⓐ Wilga Street, Paceville ☏ 21 341 100

🍴 **Jade Garden** €€ ❻ Simple but excellent oriental cuisine with attentive personal service from George, the owner. ⓐ Elia Zammit Street, Paceville ☏ 21 340 532

☕ **Il Kantina** € ❼ Rustic-style establishment in a busy location right at the head of Spinola Bay. ⓐ St George's Road ☏ 21 339 865.

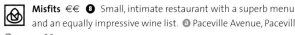

Misfits €€ **8** Small, intimate restaurant with a superb menu and an equally impressive wine list. ⓐ Paceville Avenue, Paceville ⓣ 21 331 766

Peppino's Restaurant and Wine Bar €€ **9** Excellent place for drinks or a meal, overlooking Spinola Bay. The menu ranges from seafood dishes to speciality cuisine. ⓐ St George's Road, St Julian's ⓣ 21 373 200 ⓛ Open for lunch and dinner, closed Sun

Piece of Cake € **10** Popular café, serving enormous portions of cake and ice cream, plus snacks. ⓐ 23 Wilga Street, Paceville

La Sikania € **11** Friendly, family-run establishment serving traditional Sicilian cuisine. ⓐ Paceville Avenue. Paceville ⓣ 21 339 103

Valentino €€ **12** Formal, but relaxed. Treat yourself to giant prawns in Pernod sauce, or roasted quails. ⓐ Gort Street, Paceville ⓣ 21 311 753/378 731 ⓛ Open daily, closed Sun morning

NIGHTLIFE

The Alley **13** Ever-popular rock bar with a variety of music played all night long. ⓐ Wilga St, Paceville ⓣ 21 372 246

Axis **14** Cavernous nightclub with three massive dance areas and several bars. ⓐ St George's Road, Paceville ⓣ 21 318 078 ⓛ Open daily in summer, mainly weekends only in winter ⓘ Admission charge

Dragonara Palace **15** Set in a former banker's villa. Roulette, stud poker, punto banco and black jack are played and there are 174 slot machines as well. There is also an excellent and moderately priced restaurant and bar. ⓐ At the tip of the Dragonara Point headland ⓛ Mon–Fri 10.00–06.00, and 24 hours at weekends (Oct–June); Open 24 hours (July–Sept) ⓣ 21 382 362 ⓘ Smart casual is the dress code

Bugibba & Qawra
popular holiday resorts

Together, Bugibba (pronounced 'Boo-jib-a') and Qawra (pronounced 'Aw-rah') form one of Malta's three most important holiday areas. The former consists mainly of apartments, while the latter comprises a handful of large hotels with panoramic views on to Salina Bay. Both resorts have modern, pedestrianized centres with shops, restaurants and bars catering mainly for British tastes.

At Bugibba, a long promenade runs along the waterfront overlooking the lido, offering water sports, cafés and a funfair. Nightlife is lively with numerous late-night bars and discos. Qawra is somewhat quieter, and has good water sports facilities. Amidst all the modern tourist facilities there are two remnants of the era of the Knights. The **Qawra Tower** at the tip of the peninsula was built by the Grand Master Martin de Redin in the 17th century.

At the head of **Salina Bay** is a curious expanse of shallow square depressions cut into the rock. These are salt pans carved out by the Knights in the 17th century and are still used commercially. An even older specimen of early Maltese life, a prehistoric megalith, stands in the gardens of the **New Dolmen hotel**.

 Beware the timeshare touts who operate locally, especially in and around Bugibba's central square. It is best to politely, but firmly, say 'no'.

THINGS TO SEE & DO
Empire Cinema ★★
This four-screen cinema shows the latest Hollywood films, often in English with sub-titles, and also has a wide range of electronic games.
ⓐ Pioneer Road, Bugibba.

Kennedy Memorial Grove ★

Fans of the late president may want to pay homage at this quiet yet shabby spot just off the main road. Planted in 1966, the three main species of tree are said to represent the beliefs of JFK: olives for peace, oak for strength and oleander for beauty and love of life.

Underwater Safari ★★

Jump aboard **Captain Morgan's Underwater Safari Boat**, with its specially designed glass-observation keel, for a peek into the Maltese Mediterranean (see page 87). Departs from Bugibba.

BEACHES & LIDOS

Beaches The nearest are Golden Bay, Ghajn Tuffieha and Gnejna Bay (see page 30) and Mellieha (see page 32).

Sunny Coast Popular lido where you can play tennis, use the gym or indoor pool, or simply relax on the sundeck. ⓐ Qawra Road

RESTAURANTS (see map on page 26)

Incognito €€ ❶ A good standard of Maltese and international dishes is on the menu in this highly popular restaurant-pub. Flambés are a speciality. Live music and entertainment nightly.
ⓐ Triq Il Fliegu, Qawra ⓣ 21 572 028

It-Tokk €–€€ ❷ The name means 'the meeting place' and if you want to sample authentic Maltese cuisine (rabbit, bragioli, octopus) then this really is the place to meet. Book a terrace table with views over Qawra Point. ⓐ Sol Suncrest Hotel, Qawra ⓣ 21 577 101 ext 851/699

Little Wok € ❸ This Chinese restaurant, in the heart of the resort not far from the main square, is highly recommended for its good food at reasonable prices. ⓐ Triq il-Halel, Bugibba ⓣ 21 570 528

Qawra
Point

Salina Bay

QAWRA TOWER

TRIQ IL-QAWRA

2

1

TRIQ IL FLIEGU

SALT PANS

ISLET PROMENADE

5

KENN
MEMOR
GR

9

4

7

TRIQ IT-TURISTI

6

N

3

i

FOOTBALL
GROUND

0   500m

8

TRIQ IL-KORP TAL PIJUNIERI

0   0.25 mile

EMPIRE
CINEMA

ISLET PROMENADE

TRIQ IL-MOSTA

JETTY

Savini €€€ **4** Save up for a special night out in an old Maltese farmhouse. The Italian food is anything but fast but this is a place to linger and savour. **a** Qawra Road **t** 21 576 927

Ta' Cassia €€ **5** Enjoy Maltese and continental cooking in the delightful setting of an old farmhouse courtyard. **a** Qawra Road **t** 21 571 435

NIGHTLIFE
Bugibba
Visitors to Bugibba looking for some evening entertainment can try the **Corner Pocket** (for pool and karaoke), and the American-themed **Wise Guys** (for live music).

Qawra
For nightlife in Qawra, try **Incognito**, the **Little Waster** (for football fans), **Swings** (for cocktails), the **Red Lion** (say no more), **Goodfellows** and the unpretentious **Drive-In**.

The Abyss **6** Most types of music get an airing at this likeable venue though they specialize in promoting local rock bands. **a** Triq il-Kavetta, Bugibba

Amazonia **7** A beach club converted into a series of themed bars and discos. The current 'in' place on the island. **a** The Promenade, opposite the Oracle Casino **t** 21 581 510

Club Class **8** Charts and pop music are the mainstays of Club Class. **a** Pioneer Road (below Springfields). **c** Open nightly (summer); Fri–Sun (winter)

Oracle Casino **9** This casino in the New Dolmen Hotel has a choice of play from roulette, horses, blackjack and many more. There is also a bar and restaurant. **a** Qawra **t** 21 581 510

● *St Paul's Bay*

St Paul's Bay
sunny fishing harbour

Local tradition has it that St Paul's Bay is the site where the Apostle Paul was shipwrecked while on his way to trial in Rome in AD 60. He was washed ashore, (together with St Luke) and so brought Christianity to Malta. Today the little fishing settlement of St Paul's Bay is largely unaffected by tourism, which has its focus a short distance around the bay, at Bugibba and Qawra (see page 24).

The harbour, with its bright fishing boats bobbing peacefully in the water, is one of the most picturesque spots on the island. On the shore near the town centre is the **Wignacourt Tower**, built by a Grand Master in 1610.

Out in the bay are two small islands dedicated to St Paul. The larger one boasts a statue. Both can be seen on a boat trip round the bay, which runs from the quay at Bugibba, a short walk away.

On the opposite side of the bay to St Paul's is **Xemxija** (pronounced 'Shem-shee-ya'), meaning sunny place, also with some access to the sea. Beyond is **Mistra Bay**, a secluded sandy and pebbly inlet. If you want to sunbathe, a much better idea is to visit the lovely sandy beaches of **Golden Bay** and **Ghajn Tuffieha** (see page 30) just 6 km (4 miles) east. Beware – they do get very busy in high season and at weekends. Near these beaches are the remains of prehistoric temples, the Roman Baths and the village of **Mgarr**, with its large church.

THINGS TO SEE & DO
Horse riding ★
Very friendly stables at **Golden Bay Horse Riding**, used to accommodating all standards of rider. ⓐ Golden Bay (well signposted). ☎ 21 573 360

Mgarr Church ★
This handsome baroque church is known as the Egg Church as it was funded largely by the sale of eggs from the village – hence its strange egg-shaped dome (which is best appreciated from a distance). There are a number of bars and cafés around the church square.

Mgarr Shelter ★★
Mgarr's World War II underground shelter, opened to the public in 2003, is one of the island's largest; 12 metres (39 ft) deep and more than 225 metres (738 ft) long, it was dug entirely by hand. Oddly, the entrance is through a restaurant. ⓐ Barri Restaurant, Church Square ⓛ Open Tues–Sat 09.00–14.00 and on Sun to 11.30 ☎ 21 573 235

Roman Baths ★
The remains of the steam rooms, swimming pool, hot and cold baths and mosaics uncovered at this ancient villa are proof that the pursuit of leisure has a long history on Malta. The ruins are visible through the fence, but for access, the Museums Department requires advance notice. ⓐ Just over 1.5 km (just under 1 mile) from Ghajn Tuffieha on the road to Mgarr ☎ 21 251 874

Skorba Temples ★

A Neolithic village was uncovered here, and pottery from the site can be seen in the National Museum of Archaeology in Valletta. The remnants of the two temples are contemporary with Ggantija on Gozo, thought to be the oldest free-standing structures in the world. ⓐ About 1.5 km (1 mile) east of Mgarr, on the outskirts of Zebbieh ❶ 21 222 966 ◓ Open by appointment only

BEACHES

Ghajn Tuffieha Pronounced 'Ein tuff-ee-ha', this is the island's most charming sandy cove in a beautiful natural setting, a short walk from Golden Bay beach. It is narrow, however, and soon becomes crowded.

Gnejna Bay To get to Gnejna Bay (pronounced 'Je-nay-na'), you can either walk from Ghajn Tuffieha (see above), or go the long way round, by car, via Mgarr. The reward is a sandy beach, usually quiet, with fishermen's boathouses, snacks and some water sports.

Golden Bay A beautifully located golden-sand bay in between cliffs. It is overlooked by a new hotel construction and a few snack bars but is otherwise unspoiled. Water sports available.

RESTAURANTS

Charles 'Il-Barri' € If you are driving to Gnejna Bay you will pass this renowned local restaurant in the main square of Mgarr. Its traditional rabbit dishes are rated among the best on the island. ⓐ Church Square ❶ 21 573 235 ◓ Open daily from 18.30

Gandhi Tandoori €€ Authentic Indian cooking with some interesting specials always on the menu. Best value is the weekend buffet. ⓐ Mosta Road ❶ 21 572 260 ❶ Booking is recommended

SNAKEBITE
The parish church, **St Paul's Shipwreck**, is said to be built on the spot where the Apostle was bitten by a deadly viper. Apparently unaffected, he threw the snake into the fire beside him, thus enhancing his already saintly reputation.

Gillieru €€€ One of the area's best restaurants, specializing in fish and seafood and also serving local dishes. Eat inside or, less formally on the terrace, enjoying wonderful views over the bay. ⓐ 66 Church Street ⓣ 21 573 269/573 480

Harley's Bar €€€ Prime-quality Irish beef, Barbary duck and fresh Scottish salmon are typical dishes at this English country-style pub-restaurant. ⓐ Main Road ⓣ 21 571 140

Nostalgia €€€ This is what fine dining is all about. This upscale restaurant specializes in meat dishes – their Chateaubriand is superb. ⓐ 14 Mosta Road ⓣ 21 584 866 ⓘ Reservations recommended

Porto del Sol €€€ Fish, seafood and Maltese dishes are the specialities of this upmarket restaurant. Superb location with large windows that make the most of the panoramic bay views. Sunday lunch is highly recommended. ⓐ Xemxija Road ⓣ 21 573 970

Shaukiwan €€ The best Chinese food in the area, set in a quiet and romantic location, overlooking Xemxija Bay. ⓐ Xemxija Hill ⓣ 21 573 678 ⓛ Open daily

Il Veccia €€ Traditional-style restaurant with wonderful bay views serving Maltese and international dishes. Try the rabbit or the seafood specialities. ⓐ 372 St Paul's Street ⓣ 21 582 376 ⓛ Open evenings and Sun lunch

Mellieha
white sandy beach

Mellieha Bay (pronounced 'Mell-ee-ha') is famous for its white sandy beach – easily the longest on the island, at around 600 m (650 yards). It shelves gently into the Mediterranean and is nearly always a colourful sight, with yachts and *luzzus* at anchor, while windsurfers skim the waves. The unspoilt village of Mellieha is perched high above the beach with its landmark parish church looking imperiously down on the seaside activity.

The road sweeps dramatically up from the beach to **Marfa Ridge**, the northern-most part of the island. This is good walking country, although you can also drive to the northern and southern extremities for dramatic sea views. On a clear day, the islands of **Comino** and **Gozo** seem almost within swimming distance, and side roads descend to the lesser-known beaches of **Armier Bay**, **Paradise Bay** and **Ramla Bay**. Ferries depart from Cirkewwa for the island of Gozo (see page 66).

On a summer weekend the roads to and from Mellieha are chock-a-block with Maltese beachgoers. If you want to avoid the worst of the crowds, get there early or late – most families will be leaving around 17.00, even though there is a lot of sunshine still left.

THINGS TO SEE & DO
Ghadira Bird Reserve ★★
This is a much-needed sanctuary for Malta's indigenous birds and migratory visitors (a great many of whom are often killed by the island's rapacious hunters). ● Guided tours summer weekends 09.00–16.00

● *Mellieha Bay*

Bird hunters' shelters dot Marfa Ridge and, though you may find the shooting of birds a distasteful facet of island life, it is extremely dangerous to intervene or remonstrate with the hunters.

Our Lady of the Grotto Chapel ★★

This small, cave-like chapel is one of the oldest places of worship on the island. Local legend has it that St Paul prayed here. Its frescos are said to date from the 11th century. The waters of the underground spring are said to have miraculous powers to heal childhood diseases, and the steps leading down into the grotto are lined with letters, photos and articles of baby clothing sent by people who have prayed for and received healing. ❷ Off Main Street, Mellieha

Red Tower ★★

The paintwork of the Red Tower may almost be gone, but this 17th-century structure is still a fine sight, and is occasionally open to the public. It is worth the trip for the views alone, down to the Ghadira Bird Reserve (see page 32) and the beach. ❷ Make a very sharp turn left almost at the top of the hill rising from Mellieha Beach. You can drive or walk. The route is steep, but perfectly accessible.

Selmun Palace ★

This handsome 18th-century castle-like palace has been restored and is now part of a hotel complex, though non-guests may use its high-class French restaurant. It's worth the detour just to admire its frontage.

Sweethaven Village ★★★

Built for the 1980 movie *Popeye*, starring Robin Williams, this film set, resembling a ramshackle Newfoundland fishing village, continues to pack in the crowds (though it was designed to last just a matter of months). The village was built in an extremely photogenic spot, facing a beautiful bay, with a tiny sandy beach – so pack your swimming kit, in case there is room. A small children's amusement park has also sprung up here to cater for the little ones. ☎ 21 572 430 ❶ Admission charge

BEACHES

Armier Bay This small but attractive sandy beach is used mostly by locals and may provide a less-crowded alternative when Mellieha Beach gets too busy – but don't bank on it! There is a restaurant here and some water sports are available.

Mellieha Bay (Il Ghadira) Il Ghadira means 'the swamp' but the description could hardly be more inappropriate for what many visitors consider to be Malta's finest beach. Most water sports are catered for, but the conditions particularly favour windsurfing.

Paradise Bay This lovely sandy cove lies behind the Gozo ferry terminal and is something of a secret to many visitors. On a summer weekend, however, it is packed to the gills with local people. Try to visit at other times.

Ramla Bay This sandy cove is another alternative on the north coast of the Marfa Ridge, though it often catches a swell.

The **Belleview Bakery** is famous locally for the quality of its baking. It is invaluable if you are self-catering, and always worth popping in to buy a savoury snack or a cake (no eat-in facilities). ⓐ Opposite the Selmun roundabout, on the outskirts of Mellieha

RESTAURANTS

L'Amigo Bar and Restaurant €€ A good selection of grilled or fried fish, Maltese dishes, chicken, steak, pizza and pasta. Dine upstairs on the open-air veranda. ⓐ 55 G. Borg Olivier Street ⓣ 21 520 822 ⓛ Open Mon–Sat 11.00–14.00 and 18.00–22.00, closed Sun

The Arches €€€ One of the island's finest – and most upmarket – restaurants, serving classic continental and Maltese cuisine. Save up and come here on a special occasion. ⓐ G. Borg Olivier Street ⓣ 21 523 460

Commando Bar and Restaurant €€ This small restaurant is a good place to try Maltese dishes such as *fenek* (rabbit) or *cerna* (grouper) cooked in wine and herbs. Book a day in advance if you want to try *bragioli* (meat cooked in a traditional stew). ❷ G. Borg Olivier Street, in the square beside the church ❶ 21 523 459 ❸ Open 09.00–13.30 and 19.00–22.00, closed Mon

Dynasty Restaurant €€ This modern Chinese restaurant is tucked away in the Mellieha Holiday Centre complex and is open to non-residents. ❷ Mellieha Bay, signposted from the roundabout ❶ 21 572 460 ❸ Open daily ❶ Booking is advised

Fruit de Mer €€ Large, cheerful restaurant serving fish, meats, pasta, rice and vegetarian dishes. Set menus available. ❷ Mellieha Bay Road, next to the Luna Holiday Complex ❶ 21 521 987 ❸ Open daily

Ix-Xatba Restaurant €€€ Wide choice of fish and seafood, grills, veal, rice dishes and Maltese cuisine. The restaurant is cosy and romantic, with stone walls and pillars. ❷ Mellieha Bay Road ❶ 21 521 753 ❸ Open daily from 18.00

Le Jardin Restaurant €€€ Indulge in langouste (crayfish) 'La Salita', the chef's pride, or fresh fish, grills and meat dishes at this smart restaurant. ❷ La Salita Antonin Hotel, G. Borg Olivier Street ❶ 21 520 923

Ta' Peter €€ The decor is rather bland but the Maltese food is tasty and good value. Book in advance for the three-course Maltese national dish, or choose from fresh fish, meats or a set tourist menu. ❶ 21 523 537 ❸ Open daily for lunch, dinner and Sun lunch

NIGHTLIFE

For nightlife in Mellieha, try **Waves** disco and nightclub, at the beginning of Mellieha Bay beach area.

1 NATIONAL MUSEUM OF ARCHAEOLOGY

2 GRAND MASTER'S PALACE & HOUSE OF REPRESENTATIVES

3 PRIME MINISTER'S OFFICE

4 NATIONAL MUSEUM OF FINE ARTS

5 CASA ROCCA PICCOLA

6 MARKET

FORT ST ELMO

NATIONAL WAR MUSEUM

MEDITERRANEAN CONFERENCE CENTRE / SACRA INFERMERIA / THE MALTA EXPERIENCE

LOWER BARRACCA GARDENS

Grand Harbour

TRIQ SAN PAWL

MERCHANT'S STREET

TRIQ IR-REPUBBLIKA

CHURCH OF ST PAUL'S SHIPWRECK

MANOEL THEATRE

OLD THEATRE STREET

ST JOHN'S CO-CATHEDRAL & MUSEUM

LASCARIS WAR ROOMS

CARMELITE CHURCH

OLD BAKERY STREET

UPPER BARRACC GARDENS

OLD MINT STREET

REPUBLIC STREET

LA VITTORIA

SLIEMA FERRY

Marsamxett Harbour

CITY GATE

TRITON FOUNTAIN

HASTINGS GARDENS

N

0   250   500 m

0   0.25 mile

Valletta
city of the Knights

Sir Walter Scott called Valletta 'a city built by gentlemen for gentlemen'. The gents in question were the Knights of St John, who built this wonderful city of honey-coloured stone some 430 years ago. Remarkably, it was built in just five years, following the Great Siege of 1565, as the Knights hurried to establish a new fortified capital before the next Turkish onslaught.

Valletta is named after its founder, the Grand Master Jean Parisot de la Vallette. It stretches for over half a mile along the hilly peninsula that separates the Grand Harbour and Marsamxett Harbour. The best way to appreciate the grandeur of this great walled city and its enormous bastions is on a harbour cruise (see page 85).

Valletta is easily explored on foot, as it was laid out in a grid pattern. **Republic Street** is the main central thoroughfare, running from Fort St Elmo at the tip of the peninsula to the Triton Fountain by the City Gate. Flights of stone steps worn smooth over the centuries lead up and down the steep and atmospheric side streets of the old town, which are lined with tall limestone houses sporting enclosed balconies, small shops and bars. They open on to grand central squares and shady gardens overlooking the sea.

Five of the eight original *auberges*, the palatial inns that housed the different *langues*, or nationalities, of the Order of St John, have survived.

GETTING THERE
Traffic, a one-way road system, and the difficulty of finding parking space can make driving into Valletta a frustrating experience. The easiest way to reach the city is on the five-minute ferry crossing from Sliema. All major bus routes around the island also pass through here. The Sunday market can be visited on a coach tour.

> ## THE MALTESE CROSS
> The Maltese Cross became the symbol of the Order of the Knights of St John in the mid-13th century. It is white, the colour of purity, and its four arms stand for the virtues of Justice, Fortitude, Prudence and Temperance. The eight points represent the eight *langues* of the Order, as well as the beatitudes from Christ's Sermon on the Mount.

The **Auberge de Castille et Léon**, at Castille Place, has the grandest facade and is now the office of the prime minister. The **Auberge d'Italie** in Merchants' Street has been renovated and now houses the Malta Tourism Authority, while the Auberge de Provence houses the **National Museum of Archaeology**. There are also a number of churches worth visiting, including **St Paul's Shipwreck** church, with frescoed ceilings and a relic of the saint; **La Vittoria** (Church of Our Lady of Victories), Valletta's oldest building; and the **Carmelite Church**, its massive dome a landmark of the skyline.

Valletta has its own rhythms: surging with shoppers and sightseers during the morning and late afternoon, snoozing during the siesta hours, and generally quiet in the evenings. The **Sunday market** (see page 43), near the Triton Fountain and central bus depot, attracts bargain hunters from around the island. Just beyond is the suburb of Floriana, with gardens and churches to explore.

THINGS TO SEE & DO
Fort St Elmo ★★★
An enjoyable guided tour relates the epic story of the Great Siege of 1565 and also gives you a glimpse of the grim former barracks where parts of the 1978 movie, *Midnight Express*, were filmed. 'In Guardia' (see page 12) is also staged here. ● Tours Sat 13.00–17.00, Sun 09.00–17.00 ⓘ Admission charge

---

● *Auberge de Castille, now the office of the prime minister, Valletta*

Casa Rocca Piccola ★★

This 16th-century palazzo was built for the Italian knight Pietro La Rocca, and is now the home of his descendant, the 9th Marquis de Piro, himself a modern-day Knight. Its rooms contain a rich collection of antique furniture, silver and paintings, and along with the costume museum give a fascinating insight into the customs and lifestyle of the Maltese nobility over 400 years. ⓐ 74 Republic Street ⓣ 21 231 796 ⓛ Open 10.00–16.00, tours on the hour ⓘ Admission charge

Grand Masters' Palace ★★★

Built in 1571, this splendid palace was home to the Grand Masters of the Knights for over 200 years. Today it is the office of the President of Malta and seat of the country's parliament. The Armouries hold a great collection of military hardware and a lively tour brings the State Apartments to life. ⓐ Entrance on Triq il-Merkanti ⓣ 21 221 221 ⓛ Open Mon–Sat 08.15–17.00, Sun till 16.15 (1 Oct–15 June); daily 07.45–14.00 (16 June–30 Sept) ⓘ Admission charge

Lascaris War Rooms ★

This warren of underground rooms was the island's command headquarters during World War II. Operation rooms have been re-created and a headphones tour takes you back to the dark siege days of 1942. ⓐ Lascaris Ditch ⓣ 21 234 936 ⓛ Open Mon–Fri 09.30–16.30, Sat and Sun 09.30–13.00 ⓘ Admission charge

The Malta Experience ★★★

This tourist attraction is probably the best of Malta's many audio-visual shows, providing an entertaining general introduction to the islands' history and culture. ⓐ Mediterranean Conference Centre, Mediterranean Street ⓣ 21 243 776 ⓛ Show times on the hour, Mon–Fri 11.00–16.00, Sat and Sun 11.00–13.00 ⓘ Admission charge

SHOPPING

Republic Street is the city's main shopping thoroughfare. In addition to Valletta's **Sunday market** near the City Gate, there is a daily morning market in Merchants' Street, with stalls selling clothing, accessories, CDs and cassettes. At the end of the open-air market is an indoor market hall selling foodstuffs.
🕒 Open Mon–Sat 07.00–14.00

The Artisans Centre Has a good selection of quality jewellery, prints and handicrafts. 🅐 9–10 Freedom Square, near the tourist information office 📞 21 246 216 🕒 Open Mon–Fri 09.00–13.00 and 16.00–19.00, Sat 09.00–13.00

Galea Paintings Artist Aldo Galea's prints and watercolours of Maltese scenes are unique souvenirs of the island. 🅐 8 Merchants' Street 📞 21 243 591 🕒 Open Mon–Fri 09.30–13.00 and 16.00–19.00, Sat 09.15–12.45

Gopaldas Oriental Bazaar Spread over two floors – worth a look for cheap souvenirs and gifts. 🅐 33 Republic Street 📞 21 224 938 🕒 Open Mon–Sat 09.30–19.00 and Sun 10.00–13.00 (Apr–Oct)

The Malta Government Crafts Centre Featuring Maltese handicrafts, with some items for sale. 🅐 St John's Square, opposite St John's Co-Cathedral 🕒 Open Mon–Fri 09.00–13.30 (16 June–30 Sept); Mon–Fri 09.00–12.30 and 15.00–17.00 (1 Oct–15 June)

The Silversmith's Shop Postcards from customers around the world line the walls of this shop, which produces plain and filigree silver jewellery. 🅐 218 Republic Street 📞 21 231 416 🕒 Open Mon–Fri 09.00–18.00, Sat 09.00–13.00

Manoel Theatre ★★

Built by the Knights in 1731–2, this ornate theatre with its beautiful gilded ceiling and tiered boxes was restored in 1960 and again in 2003. Attending a performance here is a treat. ⓐ Old Theatre Street ❶ 21 246389 ⓛ Guided tours Mon–Fri at 10.30, 11.30 and 16.30, Sat 11.30 and 12.30; theatre season runs Oct–May ❶ Admission charge

National Museum of Archaeology ★★★

Tells the story of Malta's remarkable prehistory and temples (which are the oldest free-standing structures in the world). ⓐ Republic Street ❶ 21 221623 ⓛ Open Mon–Sat 08.15–17.00, Sun til 16.15 (1 Oct–15 June); 07.45–14.00 (16 June–30 Sept) ❶ Admission charge

National Museum of Fine Arts ★★

Housed in a 16th-century palace, Malta's national art gallery contains paintings from the 14th to the 19th centuries, including portraits of the Grand Masters and numerous works by Mattia Preti and Antoine de Favray. The Maltese sculptor Antonio Sciortino is well represented. There is a collection of artefacts from the Knights, from medical equipment to silver, in the basement. ⓐ South Street ❶ 21 225769 ⓛ Open Mon–Sat 08.15–17.00, Sun 08.15–16.00 (1 Oct–15 June); Mon–Sun 07.45–14.00 (16 June–30 Sept) ❶ Admission charge

National War Museum ★

Among the World War II memorabilia housed in this vaulted archive beneath the ramparts of Fort St Elmo are numerous photographs, the restored Gladiator biplane *Faith*, and the George Cross which was awarded to the people of Malta in 1942. ⓐ Lower St Elmo on French Curtain ❶ 21 222 430 ⓛ Open Mon–Sat 08.15–17.00, Sun 08.15–16.00 (1 Oct–15 June); Mon–Sun 07.45–14.00 (16 June–30 Sept) ❶ Admission charge

---

◀ *Exterior statue, St John's Co-Cathedral, Valletta (see page 46)*

La Sacra Infermeria ★★

The 'Holy Infirmary' hospital was built by the knights in 1574 and reflects their original function as Knights Hospitallers, caring for sick and injured pilgrims in the Middle Ages. It is now occupied by 'The Knights Hospitallers', a series of historical tableaux on the history of the Knights. ⓐ Mediterranean Street ① 21 224 135 ○ Open Mon–Fri 09.00–16.30; Knights Hospitallers open Sat and Sun 09.30–16.00 ❶ Admission charge

St John's Co-Cathedral ★★★

Malta's second cathedral (hence Co-Cathedral) in addition to the one in Mdina. This magnificent church of the Knights was completed in 1577. The interior is a riot of colour. Don't miss the Caravaggio paintings in the Cathedral Museum. ⓐ St John's Square ① 21 225 639 ○ Open Mon–Fri 09.30–13.00 (museum closes 12.30) and 13.30–16.15, Sat 09.30–12.30 ❶ Admission charge to museum

RESTAURANTS (see map on page 38)

Blue Room €–€€ ❶ Small, air-conditioned Chinese restaurant with smart blue-and-white decor. Nice variations on the standard dishes, such as spicy seafood and tofu served in earthenware pots. ⓐ Republic Street ① 21 238 014 ○ Open noon–15.00 and 19.00–23.00

Bologna €€ ❷ One of the capital's best Italian restaurants, and particularly good value at lunch time. ⓐ 59 Republic Street ① 21 246 149 ○ Open Mon–Sat noon–14.15 and 19.00–22.15

British Hotel € ❸ The balcony of the British Hotel enjoys a wonderful view of the Grand Harbour – and the Maltese food is very good value. ⓐ St Ursula Street ① 21 224 730 ○ Open daily

Café Diva €€ ❹ Pleasant if pricey sandwich bar and café serving gourmet sandwiches, toasties, bruschettas, coffees and sweets in an airy courtyard next to the Manoel Theatre. ⓐ Old Bakery Street ❶ 21 223005 ⓛ Open Mon–Fri 09.00–15.30

Café Marquee € ❺ Great location with outdoor tables on a patio opposite St John's Co-Cathedral. Pasta, pizza, sandwiches, salads and ice-cream are among the usual café fare ⓐ St John's Square ❶ 21 236 257 ⓛ Open 09.00–19.00

Café La Veneziana € ❻ Small café, popular with the locals, serving breakfast, take-away fare and café meals, and good home-made burgers. ⓐ 29 Melita Street ❶ 21 222513 ⓛ Open 07.00–22.00, closed during siesta

Caffè Cordina €€ ❼ A city institution. Take a look inside the beautiful interior of the establishment before pulling up a chair on the square outside. ⓐ Republic Square ❶ 21 234 385 ⓛ Open 08.30–20.00

The Carriage €€€ ❽ Fine cuisine and grand views over the harbour and roof-tops of Valletta make this one of the city's best restaurants. The three-course set menu of the week features Mediterranean cooking. ⓐ 22–25 South Street (take the lift from the lobby of Valletta Buildings) ❶ 21 247 828 ⓛ Open Mon–Thurs noon–15.30, Fri and Sat 07.30–23.30

Castille Restaurant €€ ❾ Rooftop dining at the top of the Castille Hotel, with splendid views over the harbour. Maltese and Mediterranean cuisine, à la carte or set menus. Music on Friday evenings. ⓐ Castille Square ❶ 21 243 677 ⓛ Open 07.30–09.30, noon–14.30 and 19.30–22.30

La Cave € **10** This cosy wine cellar below the Castille Hotel serves pasta, pizza and cheese with wine. ⓐ Castille Square ☎ 21 243 678 ◷ Open noon–15.00 and 18.00–23.00

Eddie's Café Regina € **11** Enjoy the pizzas, pasta, grilled meats and Maltese dishes at the shady green tables in Republic Square or in the cool, air-conditioned interior. ⓐ Republic Square ☎ 21 246 454 ◷ Open 10.00–22.00

Gianinni €€€ **12** Nouvelle cuisine with an Italian bias, and magnificent views of Marsamxett Harbour. Popular with those with an expense account. Reservations essential. ⓐ 23 Windmill Street ☎ 21 237 121 ◷ Open lunch and dinner Mon–Sat (Oct–May), closed Sat lunch (June–Sept)

Jasmine €€ **13** A good range of dishes served in this small Cantonese restaurant in the market quarter. ⓐ 279 St Paul Street ☎ 21 226 078 ◷ Open 11.00–15.00

Da Lucia € **14** Pleasant little café serving good salads and coffee, pizza and snacks. ⓐ 28 South Street ☎ 21 236 258 ◷ Open Mon–Fri 08.00–20.00, Sat 08.00–13.00

Perfection Café € **15** A good selection of sandwiches, plate lunches and a choice of pasta and sauces at this simple café. Evening meals are served in winter. ⓐ 56 Old Theatre Street ☎ 21 237 992 ◷ Open 08.00–14.30 (summer); 08.00–20.30 (winter)

Scalini €€ **16** Veal dishes – along with pasta, fish and chicken – top the menu at this small Italian restaurant with simple, pleasant decor. ⓐ 32 South Street ☎ 21 246 221 ◷ Open Mon–Fri noon–14.30 and 19.00–23.00, Sat 19.00–23.00, closed Sun

◀ *Valletta's stout defences of honey-coloured stone*

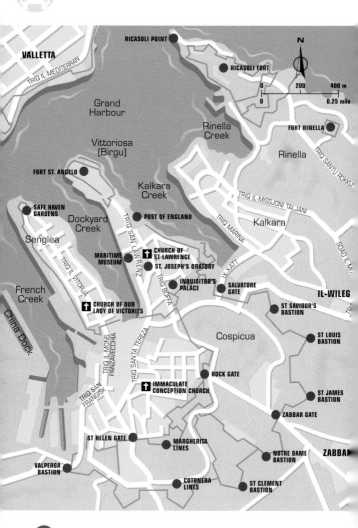

VALLETTA

TRIQ IL-MEDITERRAN

RICASOLI POINT

RICASOLI FORT

N

0   200   400 m

0   0.25 mile

Grand
Harbour

Rinella
Creek

FORT RINELLA

Vittoriosa
(Birgu)

Rinella

TRIQ SANTU ROKKU

FORT ST. ANGELO

Kalkara
Creek

TRIQ IL-MISSJONI TALJANI

SAFE HAVEN
GARDENS

Dockyard
Creek

POST OF ENGLAND

TRIQ SAN LAWRENZ

TRIQ MARINA

Kalkara

Senglea

TRIQ IL VITORJA

MARITIME
MUSEUM

CHURCH OF
ST LAWRENCE

ST. JOSEPH'S ORATORY

TRIQ BUFFA

INQUISITOR'S
PALACE

SALVATORE
GATE

IKXATT

IL-WILEG

French
Creek

CHURCH OF OUR
LADY OF VICTORIES

ST SAVIOUR'S
BASTION

China Dock

TRIQ IL-MONS
PANZAVECCHIA

TRIQ SANTA TERZA

Cospicua

ST LOUIS
BASTION

ROCK GATE

IMMACULATE
CONCEPTION CHURCH

ST JAMES
BASTION

TRIQ SAN
FRANGISK

ZABBAR GATE

ST HELEN GATE

MARGHERITA
LINES

VALPERGA
BASTION

NOTRE DAME
BASTION

ZABBAR

COTONERA
LINES

ST CLEMENT
BASTION

The Three Cities
Malta as it was

The Three Cities – Senglea, Cospicua and Vittoriosa – occupy the finger-like peninsulas jutting into the Grand Harbour from the shore opposite Valletta. They were the first base on Malta for the Knights of St John, who came here in 1530 following their expulsion from Rhodes. Dockyard Creek separates Senglea and Vittoriosa, with Cospicua linking the two on the mainland shores.

The Three Cities are some of the Malta's most historic towns, but, because they lack major hotels, restaurants and tourist facilities, visitors generally overlook them. A harbour cruise gives a tantalizing glimpse of the handsome waterfront buildings, and of the old-fashioned *dghajsas* (pronounced 'day-sas') – Malta's version of gondolas – drifting peacefully in Senglea's harbour. Anyone who returns to explore the Three Cities in more detail will be rewarded with a taste of Malta as it was in the days before mass tourism.

The Knights first established themselves at Birgu because it provided shelter for their ships. They set about fortifying the dilapidated Fort St Angelo at the tip and constructing their first auberges and palaces. By the 1560s the growing city had spread beyond the walls to form the suburb of Bormla, now known as Cospicua. Meanwhile the separate town of L'Isla, renamed Senglea after the French Grand Master Claude de la Sengle following the construction of Fort St Michael in 1552, arose on the opposite peninsula. Birgu was renamed Vittoriosa in honour of the Knights' victory over the Turks in the Great Siege of 1565, though many locals still call it by its original name. When the new capital of Valletta was built, the fortunes of the Three Cities began to decline. But, lines of defences continued to be built around them well into the 17th century.

With the development of the shipbuilding and shipping industries at nearby Marsa, dockyard workers made their homes in the Three Cities. But they also became targets for bombing raids during World War II, with Senglea and Cospicua suffering extensive damage.

THINGS TO SEE & DO
COSPICUA

Like neighbouring Senglea, Cospicua was heavily bombed during
World War II and there is little to see in its narrow, stepped streets.
The ornate Church of the Immaculate Conception, built in 1637, is one
of the few buildings to have escaped destruction and is worth a look.
The city is enclosed by a double ring of bastions, the landward
defences built by the Knights. The inner Margherita Lines, with six
bastions, were begun in 1639. Between 1670 and 1680, the Cotonera
Lines, funded by Grand Master Nicolas Cotoner, were built beyond.
The Zabbar Gate is the best of the finely carved triumphal gateways
that break the curtain walls.

Fort Rinella ★

Fort Rinella, built by the British in the 19th century, lies north east of the
Three Cities. It contains an enormous gun and historical re-enactments
take place on the last Sunday of certain months. 🕒 Open Mon–Sat
10.00–17.00, Sun 13.00–17.00 (Oct–May); 10.00–13.00 daily (June–Sept)
🛈 Admission charge

SENGLEA

Senglea was heavily bombed during World War II. Victory Street, the
main thoroughfare, runs from the main square to the gardens on the
peninsula. There is also an attractive waterfront along Dockyard Creek.

Church of Our Lady of Victories ★

The church, in the main town square, was badly damaged in the bombing
but is now restored to its former glory, with a fine, painted dome.

Safe Haven Gardens ★★

Also called Gardjola Garden, these gardens surround the picturesque
Vedette, or lookout post, on the tip of the peninsula and offer superb
panoramic views of the entire Grand Harbour. The *vedette* is a six-sided
tower, finely carved with two eyes and two ears to signify vigilance

THE GREAT CHAIN

The Knights had a secret weapon for defending the Three Cities during the Great Siege. An enormous chain, which had been forged in Venice, was strung across the entrance to Dockyard Creek between Senglea and Fort St Angelo. A remnant can still be seen below the fort.

against enemy ships. It is one of the few survivors of pre-World War II Senglea. The gardens were created on the site of Fort St Michael, which was built by the Knights and dismantled by the British to create docks for the Royal Navy.

VITTORIOSA

Vittoriosa has a fine old town centre and is the most atmospheric of the Three Cities. A stroll along its narrow, winding streets reveals many delights, such as the lovely architecture of Victory Square, which is surrounded by the *auberges* of England, Germany and Auvergne et Provence. The three elegant gateways at the landward side of the city – Advanced Gate, Couvre Porte and Provence Gate – were built in the early 18th century. The Post of England lookout on the Kalkara Creek side has views of the former Bighi Naval Hospital and the old Ricasoli Fort on adjacent peninsulas.

Church of St Lawrence ★

This landmark of Vittoriosa's waterfront, with its dome and twin clock towers, is a 17th-century reconstruction of the Knights' original Conventual Church. The interior is richly decorated with red marble, frescos and an outstanding painting, the *Martyrdom of St Lawrence* by Mattia Preti. In front of the church, the Freedom Monument commemorates the British withdrawal from Malta in 1979. ⓐ St Lawrence Street ⓞ 21 827 057 ⓛ Open Mon–Sun 06.00–10.00 and 16.00–19.00

Fort St Angelo ★

The Knights fortified an earlier castle on this strategic point and from here they repelled the Turks during the Great Siege. The first Grand Masters and many Knights are buried here. It later became a prison and was a naval base for the Allies during World War II. ● Guided tours every 15 minutes, Sat 09.00–13.00 (June–Sept); 10.00–14.00 (Oct–May) ● Admission charge

The Inquisitors' Palace ★★

Built in 1574, this palace was the headquarters of the Inquisition in Malta. Gruesome tortures took place here, as the hated Inquisitors sought to extract 'confessions' of heresy. The museum contains furniture and household goods. You can also visit the court room, main hall, chapel and dungeons, where the prisoners' graffiti is still visible. ● Main Gate Street ● 21 827 006 ● Open Mon–Sun 07.45–14.00 (summer); Mon–Sat 08.15–16.30, Sun 08.15–16.00 (winter) ● Admission charge.

The Maritime Museum ★★

Malta's naval history is illustrated with photos, models of the galleys of the Knights and of traditional Maltese fishing vessels, and even medieval navigation tools. ● Dockyard Creek ● 21 660 052 ● Open Mon–Sun 07.45–14.00 (summer); Mon–Sat 08.15–17.00, Sun 08.15–16.00 (winter) ● Admission charge

MEDITERRANEAN FILM STUDIOS

On the coast to the north of Vittoriosa is a unique film set. Two huge seawater tanks have been designed to show the sky as a natural backdrop, allowing film-makers to safely shoot realistic ocean scenes. One is used for surface shots and the other for underwater scenes. Many films and TV series, such as *Howards' Way*, *Christopher Columbus*, *Gladiator*, *The Count of Monte Cristo* and *Troy* have been filmed here.

● *Vittoriosa's waterfront landmark, the Church of St Lawrence*

St Joseph's Oratory ★★

Built as a chapel behind the church of St Lawrence in the 18th century, the oratory is now a small museum containing artefacts brought by the Knights from Rhodes. Grand Master Jean de la Vallette's hat and sword, and a crucifix used at executions are here. ⓐ Vittoriosa Square ⓛ Open Mon– Sat 08.30–noon and 14.00–16.00, Sun 09.30–noon

Medieval Mdina
Malta's ancient capital

Malta's old capital is the island's most perfectly preserved medieval town. It is a world away from noisy modern-day resort life and even the gentle bustle of Valletta is a comparative cacophony. Here in the quiet narrow streets and alleyways, you can almost touch the sense of history.

The Romans were the first to settle in this area, attracted, like their successors, by its strategic situation: high inland, easy to defend and surrounded by fertile agricultural countryside. But if the name Mdina (pronounced 'Im-deena') sounds Arabic then that is not surprising. It derives from the word *medina*, meaning 'the City' and was so named by the Arabs who conquered Malta in 870 and stayed for two centuries, making the city their stronghold and capital.

Sadly, there is virtually nothing left from this period and it was left to the Knights of St John to give Mdina its current form. They fortified the city, made it their cavalry headquarters and called it Citta Notabile, meaning 'The Eminent City'. The Knights did not stay long however. After the Great Seige of 1565 they moved to Valletta and so the demise of Mdina began. It became known as the 'Old City' and as it began to fade away quietly, was renamed the 'Silent City'.

Thanks to tourism, Mdina is no longer silent, by day at any rate. Restaurants, shops and a handful of attractions draw visitors, and residents' own motor vehicles disturb the slumber (though no other vehicles are allowed in). At night, however, the city's 400 or so inhabitants enjoy what must be the quietest sleep in all Malta. A visit after dark, when the empty, dimly lit streets fall totally silent, is highly recommended.

The entrance to the city is through the splendid Main Gate, built in 1724, which lies across a bridge spanning the dry moat. The three statues on the inside facade are St Publius, St Paul and St Agatha, Malta's three patron saints. Nearly all of Mdina's sightseeing interest lies along the

▲ *Main Gate, Mdina*

main street, Triq Villegaignon. Walk slowly and gaze upwards to admire the facades of the various *palazzi* (mansions) along here. The most eminent address is the Casa Inguanez, the home of Malta's oldest aristocratic family.

BASTION SQUARE

🔵11
🔵4
🔵3
🔵6
TRIQ VILLEGAIGNON
🔵10 ST ROQUE
✝ CATHEDRAL

CARMELITE CONVENT ✝
ST PAUL'S SQUARE
🔵9
🔵8
CATHEDRAL MUSEUM
✝ ST PETER
🔵7
🔵6
MESQUITA STREET
BENEDICTINE ST PETER'S ✝ 🔵5
✝ ST NICHOLAS
MESQUITA SQUARE
Mdina
🔵5
🔵1
🔵4

GREEK'S GATE SQUARE
IGUANEZ STREET
🔵2
🔵3

🔵2

OLD RAILWAY STATION
🔵11
🔵1

MTARFA ROAD

ROMAN VILLA AND MUSEUM
🔵

MUSEUM ESPLANADE
MUSEUM ROAD
HOWARD GARDENS

✉

🚌

DONI STREET
✝ TA DONI CHURCH
THE SAQQAJJI

🔵7
ST AUGUSTINE'S STREET
SAQQAJJA

1 MDINA GATE

2 MDINA DUNGEON

3 VILHENA PALACE / MUSEUM OF NATURAL HISTORY

4 CORTE CAPITANALE

5 XARA PALACE

6 MDINA EXPERIENCE

7 CASA TESTAFERRATA

8 PALAZZO SANTA SOPHIA

9 KNIGHTS OF MALTA

10 MEDIEVAL TIMES

11 PALAZZO FALZON

ST PAUL'S STREET
✝ TA GESU CHURCH
Rabat
MAIN STREET
HOSPITAL STREET
NIKOL SAURA STREET

✝ FRANCISCAN CHURCH

VICTORY STREET
🔵10
🔵

PARISH SQUARE
✝ ST PAUL'S PARISH CHURCH
COLLEGE ST

BUSKETT ROAD

🔵8
ST AGATHA'S STREET

ST AGATHA'S CATACOMBS ↓
ENTRANCE TO ST PAUL'S CATACOMBS

THINGS TO SEE & DO

Bastion Square ★★

At the end of Triq Villegaignon, Bastion Square makes the perfect end
to a stroll through Mdina. From the city walls there are sweeping views
across the plains below. Even on the dullest day the giant dome of
Mosta's church is a mighty landmark and you should be able to see all
the way to Valletta and almost right along both coasts to St Paul's Bay
in the north and to Marsascala in the south.

Cathedral ★★★

Built in 1697–1702 by Lorenzo Gafa after the earlier church was
destroyed by an earthquake, St Paul's Cathedral is second only to
St John's Co-Cathedral in Valletta in grandeur. The rich baroque interior
is one of the finest on Malta; the vaulted ceiling is adorned with frescos
by Mattia Preti while colourful funerary slabs cover the floor. Other
highlights include the high altar of marble and lapis lazuli, and a
Byzantine icon of the Madonna and Child in a side chapel. 🅰 St Paul's
Square 🕿 21 454 136 🕒 Open Mon–Sat 09.30–11.45 and 13.30–16.30,
Sun 15.00–16.30 🛈 Donation

Cathedral Museum ★★

Housed in an 18th-century baroque palace, this museum includes more
than the usual prosaic collection of church plate and features numerous
works of art, some by famous Old Masters. The highlight is the collection
of woodcuts by Albrecht Dürer depicting the Small Passion of Christ and
the Life of the Virgin. 🅰 St Paul's Square. 🕿 21 454 697 🕒 Open Mon–Fri
10.00–17.15, Sat 10.00–15.15 🛈 Admission charge

The Knights of Malta ★

Located in historic gunpowder vaults, these tableaux depict the life
and times of the Knights with appropriate sound effects.
🅰 14–19 Magazine Street 🕿 21 451 342 🕒 Open Mon–Sat 10.30–16.30
🛈 Admission charge

Mdina Dungeon ★★

Some of the scenes in here may look like pure dark fantasy but these are real dungeons and what you see is an exhibition of real medieval Maltese horror – everything portrayed here actually happened (though not necessarily in these dungeons). If you are squeamish or you have young children in tow, give it a miss. ⓐ St Publius Square, just inside the Main Gate ⓣ 21 450267 ⓛ Open 09.30–17.30 ⓘ Admission charge

The Mdina Experience ★★

This audio-visual show in a comfortable air-conditioned auditorium gives a good general introduction to the history of the city. There is a café on site. ⓐ 7 Mesquita Square ⓣ 21 454 322 ⓛ Open Mon–Fri 10.30–16.00, Sat 10.30–14.00 ⓘ Admission charge

Medieval Times ★

Compared with the dungeons, this is a rather humdrum series of tableaux depicting medieval life in Malta. ⓐ In the Palazzo Notabile, Triq Villegaignon ⓣ 21 454 625 ⓛ Open Mon–Sat 10.00–16.30 ⓘ Admission charge

Museum of Natural History ★

The handsome 18th-century Vilhena Palace is home to Mdina's old-fashioned natural history museum. It is dry in tone as some of the bones it displays, but worth a visit. ⓐ St Publius Square, adjacent to the Mdina Dungeon. ⓣ 21 455 951 ⓛ Open Mon–Sun 07.45–14.00 (16 June–30 Sept); Mon–Sat 08.15–17.00, Sun 08.15–16.15 (1 Oct–15 June) ⓘ Admission charge

Palazzo Falzon ★

Also known as the Norman House; this 14th-century mansion contains a small museum of naval art and antique furniture. ⓐ Triq Villegaignon ⓣ 21 454 512 ⓛ Open Mon–Fri 10.30–13.00 and 14.30–16.30 ⓘ Donation

The Mdina Art Gallery displays lovely works by the Maltese artist Marco Cremona. Prints of his Maltese scenes are for sale, along with other local arts and crafts. ❷ Mesquita Square

RESTAURANTS (see map on page 58)

AD 1530 € ❶ Bright trattoria serving pizza, pasta, salads and light snacks. ❷ Adjacent to the Xara Palace Hotel ☎ 21 450 560

Bacchus €€ ❷ Two chambers of a 17th-century gunpowder magazine in a fortified bastion of the town walls make a unique setting for one of Mdina's best restaurants. Speciality fish dishes, grills, pasta, soups and salads are on the menu. ❷ Inguanez Street ☎ 21 454 981 ◷ Open 09.00–21.00

Ciappetti € ❸ Charming courtyard restaurant serving Italian specialities, with a terrace upstairs on the bastion. ❷ 5 St Agatha's Esplanade ☎ 21 459 987 ◷ Open 11.00–15.30 and 19.30–23.00

Fontanella € ❹ Only the selection of scrumptious homemade cakes can out-do the view at this terrace café along the ramparts near Bastion Square. Sandwiches and salads are also available. ❷ 1 Bastion Street ☎ 21 454 264 ◷ Open 10.00–22.00 (summer); 10.00–18.00 (winter)

De Mondion €€€ ❺ Elegant dining is offered in the roof-garden restaurant of the Xara Palace Hotel. The table d'hôte menu features French and Mediterranean cuisine, with dishes such as Maltese baby pig, sea bass fillet and potato gnocchi. ❷ Xara Palace Hotel ☎ 21 450 560 ◷ Open 19.30–22.30 ❶ Booking is advised

Palazzo Notabile €€ ❻ This trattoria enjoys a beautiful setting in a 17th-century baroque palace. Mediterranean and Italian cuisine including Maltese dishes. ❷ Triq Villegaignon ☎ 21 454 625 ◷ Open Mon–Sat 10.00–16.00 and 19.00–22.30, Sun 10.00–16.00

Rabat
early Christian catacombs

Rabat, meaning 'the suburb' in Arabic, lies just outside Mdina's city walls. The two were one city in Roman times, and became separated when the Arabs began building smaller fortifications around Mdina. Rabat has always acted as the commercial quarter for the old capital and continues to be a lively market town with plenty of historical interest.

Rabat is a sprawling town with some 13,000 residents, a commercial hub for much of central Malta. Its main sights, however, are all located around the central Parish Square, about a ten-minute walk from Mdina's main gate. There is a fruit and vegetable market in the square on weekdays. Few concessions to tourism impinge on the local character of Rabat, and its streets are lined with old-style houses with ornate, enclosed balconies. A multitude of saints' statues atop their wooden plinths line the streets during the annual summer *festa*.

Rabat is most famous for its early Christian **catacombs** (underground tunnels with niches for tombs). Below the streets lie a labyrinth of these underground tunnels, covering more than 2.5 square km (a square mile) in area. Malta's catacombs, unlike those in Rome, were not hiding places for persecuted Christians. They were used solely as burial chambers, and pagans and Jews were also interred here. There are various types of tombs: floor graves; canopy tombs; and small graves, known as *loculi*, cut into the wall to hold the body of a child.

The most unusual feature of the catacombs is the circular agape tables, which were carved out of the rock so that relatives of the dead could gather underground for ritual funeral and anniversary feasts with their departed loved ones. Two sets of catacombs are open to the public.

❍ *See the baroque majesty of St. Paul's, Rabat's parish church*

THINGS TO SEE & DO

Roman Villa and Museum of Roman Antiquities ★

Apart from the mosaic floor, little is left of the old Roman villa, but the museum built on site contains a collection of *amphorae* (ancient Roman jars), glass, oil lamps, and olive crusher and other artefacts. ⓐ Museum Esplanade ❶ 21 454 125 ● Open Mon–Sat 08.15–17.00, Sun 08.15–16.15 (1 Oct–15 June); daily 07.45–14.00 (16 June–30 Sept)

St Agatha's Catacombs ★★

These catacombs, dedicated to the Sicilian martyr St Agatha, are outstanding for their late Roman and medieval frescos, dating from the 3rd to 5th centuries. A guide points out the highlights on a tour lasting 20–30 minutes. You can browse through the convent's small museum, with an eclectic collection of minerals, pottery, ancient statuettes and other artefacts. ⓐ St Agatha Street ❶ 21 454 503 ● Open Mon–Fri 09.00–noon and 13.00–17.00, Sat 09.00–13.00 ❶ Admission charge

St Paul's Catacombs ★★

Malta's largest catacombs once contained some 1400 graves. You can wander through the eerie maze of lighted passages on your own. ⓐ St Agatha Street ❶ 21 454 562 ● Open Mon–Fri 08.15–17.00, Sun 08.15–16.00 (1 Oct– 15 June); daily 07.45–14.00 (16 June–30 Sept) ❶ Admission charge

St Paul's Church and Grotto ★

Rabat's parish church dates from the 16th century. The Grotto of St Paul lies beneath the adjoining Chapel of St Publius and is reached by a separate entrance. According to local tradition, St Paul took shelter here for several months following his shipwreck on Malta while he preached Christianity to the islanders. The grotto walls supposedly have healing powers. Behind the large marble statue of the saint are a series of catacombs. ⓐ Parish Square ❶ 21 454 467 ● Open 09.15–13.30 and 14.00–17.00 ❶ Donation

Also on St Agatha Street is the Empire Craft Centre – a good place to shop for lace, embroidery and other island specialities.

RESTAURANTS (see map, in Medieval Mdina, on page 58)

Cuckoo's Nest Tavern € ❼ This tiny restaurant only has a handful of tables but contains loads of atmosphere. Its speciality is *timpana*, a Maltese favourite, with layers of macaroni, meat, cheese, vegetables and eggs baked in pastry. ❸ 9 St Paul's Street ❶ 21 455 946 ❶ Open 11.30–14.30 and 19.00–22.00

Grapes € ❽ Maltese dishes and homemade wine are among the offerings at this simple, pleasant restaurant near the catacombs. There's also a snack menu. ❸ St Agatha Street ❶ 21 450 483 ❶ Open Mon–Sat 11.00–15.00 and 18.30–22.00 (23.00 on Sat)

Point de Vue € ❾ The menu at this tourist restaurant ranges from chicken, chips and omelettes to tasty Maltese dishes such as marinated lamb. The set meals are good value. ❸ 5 The Saqqajja, located outside the Mdina gate ❶ 21 454 117 ❶ Open 09.00–23.30

Ristorante Cosmana Navarra €€ ❿ Dishes range from *confit* of duck, rabbit stew, and fish in the upstairs restaurant, to snacks in the downstairs bar. ❸ 28 St Paul's Street, situated opposite the church. ❶ 21 450 638 ❶ Open Mon–Sat 18.30–22.00; bar open daily until midnight

Stazzjon Restaurant €€ ⓫ A theme restaurant set in the former railway station of the old train route that ran between Rabat and Valletta until 1931. Order your drinks at the ticket window and dine in the waiting room or on the platform in summer. The menu features grilled meats, fish and pasta. ❸ Mtarfa Road ❶ 21 451 717 ❶ Open Sat and Sun only

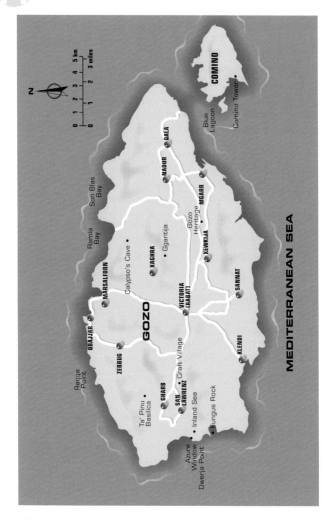

Gozo
where time stands still

Legend has it that Gozo is the legendary island of Calypso, the sea nymph who, in Homer's *Odyssey*, kept Odysseus captive for seven years. You may not stay that long, but you will most certainly feel the ancient attraction of the island's temples, standing stones and time-worn landscapes.

Many visitors wrongly assume that Gozo is just an extension of its larger sister, Malta. Though its villages are built from the same honey-coloured limestone, Gozo has a completely different feel. Guest accommodation is primarily in holiday apartments, farmhouses and upmarket hotels rather than in large resorts, so the atmosphere is quieter and the pace is slower. Gozo is Malta's market garden, and the landscape here is noticeably greener, especially in the sun-baked summer. The hill-sides and valleys are covered with fertile orchards and terraced fields that are still worked using traditional methods. On the north coast, near **Reqqa Point**, people harvest sea salt from the salt pans as their ancestors have done for centuries.

Gozo's capital, **Victoria**, lies roughly in the centre of the island and a visit to its historic citadel is a must. The hilltop towns of **Nadur**, **Xaghra** (pronounced 'Shah-ruh') and **Zebbug**, with their prominent church domes, are known as the 'three hills' because they are the island's original settlements. The fishing villages of **Marsalforn** and **Xlendi** (pronounced 'Shlen-di'), set around attractive bays, have developed as the main resorts for tourists.

Diving and swimming are excellent in the clear blue waters around Gozo's coastline. There are also good walks, both along the coast and inland. Although the island is small – only 64 sq km (26 sqmiles) – there are enough places of interest to keep you busy for a fortnight. However, Gozo is not meant for rushing around, but for relaxing on its idyllic bays, sipping a coffee or a beer at its local bars and cafés, or enjoying a meal at

▲ *Victoria Square, Xaghra, with its parish church*

its pleasant restaurants. For details of how to get to Gozo see the tip box, below. You'll need to hire a car to get the best out of the island or, if you are just visiting for a day, you can take a Gozo Excursion tour (available at most resorts, or ask at the tourist office).

The ferry crossing from Cirkewwa on Malta to Mgarr on Gozo takes about 25 minutes. In high season the 09.45 crossing can be very busy with coach-tour passengers, so queue up early if you want a seat. If you are bringing a car, these spaces can fill up quickly, especially at weekends, so get there early. In bad weather ferries may leave from Sa Maison, near Valletta, or not run at all. Call first to check.
☎ 21 243 964/5/6

THINGS TO SEE & DO
The Azure Window ★★★
Eroded limestone has never been so spectacular as at Gozo's aptly named Azure Window at Dwejra Bay. Behind it, reached by a tunnel, is the saltwater lake known as the Inland Sea. If you can watch the

sunset from here it will be a highlight of your holiday. Nearby is the offshore outcrop known as Fungus Rock, so called because of a spongy plant, *fungus melitensis*, that grew there. It was used to cure stomach pains and to stem the flow of blood from injuries, and was so prized by the Knights that they built Qawra Tower opposite to guard the supply.

Ta'Pinu Basilica ★★★

Ta'Pinu has been the national holy of holies since 1883, when the voice of the Virgin was heard in the original church that stood on this spot. The present grand basilica was built over that church in 1920. A room to the side of the main altar is filled with votive offerings in thanksgiving for the many miracles attributed to this holy place. ❸ On the outskirts of the village of Gharb ❶ 21 556 992

Gozo Heritage ★★

This attraction tells the history of Gozo, from the earth-mother symbols found in the ancient temples to the coming of Christianity through St Paul and the Knights of St John. ❸ On Mgarr Road, Ghajnsielem ❶ 21 561 280 ❷ Open Mon–Sat 08.45–16.45 ❶ Admission charge

Gozo Princess ★★

If there is time in the holiday, it is certainly a day well spent to cruise around Gozo, Comino and the Blue Lagoon on this luxury craft, with time for swimming and snorkelling. A sunset cruise is also available.
Xlendi Pleasure Cruises ❸ Departs from Xlendi ❶ 21 559 967 ❾ www.xlendicruises.com ❶ Admission charge

Ggantija ★★★

Along with Malta's other ancient temples, these 5000-year-old remains are the Earth's oldest free-standing structures, pre-dating even the Pyramids and Stonehenge. ❸ Located on the outskirts of Xaghra ❶ 21 553 194 ❷ Open Mon–Sat 08.30–16.30, Sun 08.30–13.00 (Oct–Mar); Mon–Sat 08.30–18.30 (08.30–19.00 mid-June–mid-Sept), Sun 08.30–15.00 (April–Sept) ❶ Admission charge

⬤ *Gozo's capital, Victoria, has numerous backstreets*

Gharb Folklore Museum ★★
All kinds of interesting commercial and domestic bygones are displayed in a beautifully restored 18th-century house. Definitely worth a visit.
🚌 99 Church Square, Gharb 📞 21 561 929 🕐 Open Sat 09.00–16.00, Sun 09.00–13.00 ❶ Admission charge

Marsalforn ★★
Gozo's largest resort sits in a wide bay with its colourful fleet of traditional *luzzus* (pronounced 'lut–sues') sheltered in a tiny harbour next to the small sandy beach. There are good waterfront restaurants and bars, a promenade, water sports and bicycle hire. The salt pans along the shore to the west of the village are a unique sight.

Xlendi ★★
The small resort of Xlendi, situated around a little harbour and beach below the hills, has great atmosphere, its promenade lined with restaurants, bars and shops.

VICTORIA (see map on page 72)
The island's tiny capital was named in honour of Queen Victoria's diamond jubilee in 1897 (locals still use the old name, Rabat). Independence Square (also known as It-Tokk, which means 'the meeting place') is a charming spot with trim shady trees, old-fashioned shops, a handful of cafés (don't miss Café Jubilee) and a morning market. Just off the square, the 17th-century Church of St George is known as the 'Golden Basilica' on account of its rich gilded baroque interior. The medieval lanes behind the square are fun to explore.

The citadel and cathedral ★★★
The walled citadel perched above the streets of Victoria dates back to Roman times and was fortified by the Knights of St John in the early 17th century. The panoramic views over the island from the ramparts are stupendous. Behind its rather plain facade, the cathedral is a baroque gem with a most unusual feature: when the funds ran

out to complete the planned dome, the Italian artist, Antonio Manuele, painted a *trompe-l'oeil* dome. It was probably the only parish church on Gozo for several centuries.

Housed within the citadel precincts are five small museums, the best of which is the charming **Folklore Museum**. The Archaeological Museum, Cathedral Museum, Natural History Museum and Knights' Armoury are also here. ☎ 21 556 087 (cathedral) ☎ 21 230 711 (all museums) 🕐 Museums open Mon–Sat 08.30–18.30 (08.30–19.00 mid-June– mid-Sept), Sun 08.30–15.00 ❶ Admission charge

Gozo 360 ★★

An entertaining audio-visual introduction to the island. ⓐ Citadel Theatre ☎ 21 559955 🕐 Show times every half-hour Mon–Sat 10.00–15.30, Sun 10.00–13.00 ❶ Admission charge

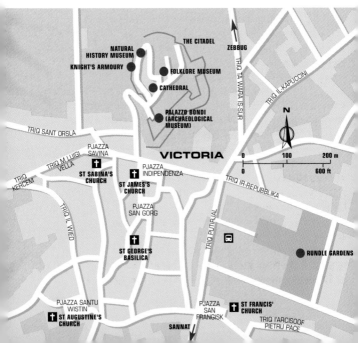

In the summer months many of the island's older women sit on their doorsteps chatting with their neighbours while their nimble fingers produce beautiful and intricate lace goods for Gozo's cottage industry. The village of Sannat is one place where you are likely to see them at work.

BEACHES

Dahlet Qorrot Set around a little harbour backed by colourful fishermen's huts, this small sandy beach is popular with local families. There is also a very good coastal walk from here to Qala Point.

Hondoq ir-Rummien This small sandy beach below the village of Qala faces the island of Comino. It is good for children but can get very crowded at weekends.

Ramla Bay This wide stretch of soft reddish sand is Gozo's best beach but thankfullly, it remains surprisingly uncrowded. Approach it on the road from Marsalforn. Above the beach is the fabled Calypso's Cave, now reduced by rock falls to a mere cleft in the rock, but a vantage point for a picture-postcard view.

San Blas This is the best little sandy cove in Gozo. It's quite a trek getting down to it and an even longer one climbing back up, but if you're fit and child-free, the good swimming here makes the effort well worthwhile.

RESTAURANTS

L'Ankra €€ You can watch the boats coming and going from the big windows of this restaurant overlooking Mgarr Harbour. Fresh fish, pasta and local specialities. ❸ 11 Shore Street, Mgarr ❶ 21 555 656 🕒 Open for lunch and dinner

Brookies Pub & Restaurant €€ Family-run restaurant situated beneath the walls of the citadel. The fish is very good. Pasta and

local dishes are also on the menu. ⓐ 1–2 Wied Sara Street, Victoria, on the main road to Zebbug ❶ 21 559 524 ❺ Open for lunch and dinner, closed Tues

 Café Jubilee € The terrace tables here make a good spot for coffee, drinks and to sample the local *ftiras* (bread with olive oil, tomato paste and tuna) or the deep-fried Gozo cheese. ⓐ Independence Square, Victoria

Chez Amand €€ This delightful bistro and restaurant, with a cool terrace overlooking the beach, serves delicious Maltese

SHOPPING

Handmade lace is a Gozitan speciality and highly prized for its quality. Shawls, tablecloths, handkerchiefs and other items are good value here. Thick, woolly Aran-style jumpers are another popular item. The small peppery rounds of *gbejniet*, Gozo's tasty sheep's-milk cheese, are sold in jars and will keep for weeks; you can buy them in the shops or market in Victoria.

Fontana Cottage Industry Sells overpriced lace, woven goods and knitwear, but you can also watch demonstrations here. ⓐ Xlendi Road in Victoria

Gozo Glass You can watch the artisans at work before buying. ⓐ Just outside Gharb on the road to Victoria ❶ 21 561 974

Ta'Dbiegi Crafts Village Set in a former army barracks, has workshops selling filigree jewellery, lace, woven and leather goods. ⓐ Near San Lawrenz ❶ 21 556 202 ❺ Open 08.30–18.45

Triq Ta'Bieb L-Imdina Local craft workshops selling jewellery, lace, candles and artcrafts. ⓐ A small lane in Victoria alongside the cathedral in the citadel

specialities and Mediterranean dishes, such as *gbejniet* (cheese) salad, seafood *amandine* and *canneloni thermidor*. A friendly spot run by Belgian chef Amand and his daughter Caroline. ❸ Qbajjar Bay, Marsalforn ❶ 21 561 188 ❺ Closed Wed (July–Sept); dinner only on Fri and Sat (Nov–Mar)

Ic-Cima €€ The terrace of this romantic restaurant overlooking Xlendi harbour is a great place to watch the sunset. Excellent pasta and pepper steak. ❸ St Simon Street, Xlendi ❶ 21 558 407 ❺ Open daily for lunch and dinner

Jeffrey's €€€ Excellent *bragioli* and other Maltese specialities are served in this old farmhouse setting with local artworks on display; you can also dine outside in the courtyard. ❸ 10 Gharb Road, Gharb. ❶ 21 561 006 ❺ Open Mon–Sat 19.00–22.00

Moby Dick's €€ The large terrace, set on the waterfront, is a great place to watch the action in the harbour over lunch or drinks. The ground-floor restaurant serves good pizzas; upstairs are the Huang Gong Chinese restaurant and the roof-garden restaurant. ❸ 4 Marina Street, Xlendi Bay ❶ 21 561 518 ❺ Open 0800–midnight or 01.00

Oleander € Experience the real taste of Gozo in a pleasant but unpretentious local diner in the centre of this pretty village. ❸ Victory Square, Xaghra ❶ 21 557 230 ❺ Open 11.30–15.00 and 18.30–22.00, closed Mon

Il-Panzier €€€ This small, intimate restaurant has courtyard dining, and is located in the back streets behind It-Tokk. The friendly owner will help match wines to the delicious Sicilian food. ❸ 5 Charity Street, behind St George's Basilica, Victoria ❶ 21 559 979 ❺ Open noon–15.00 and 19.00–23.00, closed Tues

> **LOST FOR WORDS**
> Edward Lear, the great English nonsense poet, so loved the island that he was moved to declare it 'pomskizillious and gromphiberous, being as no words can describe its magnificence'.

Salvina €€ A beautifully restored rustic house serving excellent island dishes. ⓐ 21 Triq il-Blata, Gharb ⓣ 21 552 505 ⓛ Open noon–15.00 and 18.00–22.00; dinner only in summer, closed Thurs all day

Stone Crab €€ Some of the best fish on Gozo can be had at this waterside restaurant. Carnivores can tuck into an excellent steak rossini. ⓐ Xlendi Bay ⓣ 21 559 315 ⓛ Open lunch and dinner (April–Oct); Sat and Sun only (Nov and Feb–March), closed Dec–Jan

Xerri Il-Bukkett € Gorgeous views over Mgarr harbour to Comino and Malta are to be had from the terrace of this hilltop bar and restaurant. The local *bocci* (a game like *boules*) club is adjacent to the bar. ⓐ Zewwieqa Road, Qala ⓣ 21 553 500 ⓛ Open daily

NIGHTLIFE

Victoria has two opera houses, the **Aurora** and the **Astra**, built by its rival philharmonic societies, and frequently used as cinemas. Gozo also has two nightclubs, **La Grotta** and **Paradiso**, in the countryside between Victoria and Xlendi. They get lively from 23.00 until the early hours.

◉ *Colourful buses from the island's public transport system*

Comino
the Blue Lagoon

Midway between Malta and Gozo, and covering just 2.5 square km (one square mile), Comino is the smallest of Malta's inhabited islands. It takes its name from the herb, cumin, which grew wild here in former times. Once a pirate haven, the island is now home to an away-from-it-all hotel specializing in water sports, plus a handful of farmers who somehow eke a living from this barren, sun-baked rock. There are no roads and no cars. Some tours allow you to explore the island, though there is little to see, apart from the hotel, an ancient chapel and the Santa Marija watch-tower, (which doubled as the Chateau d'If in the 2002 movie *The Count of Monte Cristo*), built by the Knights in the early 17th century. Surprisingly, this tiny spot has a police station, and mass is held once a week in the old chapel.

Comino's great attraction is the Blue Lagoon. Its heavenly turquoise waters above a seabed of soft white sand are fantastic for swimming and snorkelling, and the underwater caves and grottos are perfect for scuba divers. However, the tiny cove can become very crowded with day-trippers and cruise-boat passengers. If you want to swim, stick to the lagoon as there are jellyfish in the harbour and their stings can be quite painful. On the opposite shore is the uninhabited rock islet of Cominotto.

Most people visit Comino as part of a day cruise from Malta or Gozo. In summer there are also small boats that ferry passengers on the 15-minute trip to the Blue Lagoon from Cirkewwa harbour several times a day; from Gozo the ten-minute ferry trip operates on a regular basis.

If you decide to explore Comino, take plenty of water, a hat and extra sun cream, as there is little shade. The hotel is closed in winter, so bring food and drink as well if you visit then.

◀ *The Blue Lagoon*

Malta panorama
the centre and south east

The centre of the island holds much of interest, and a day away from the resorts will do much to round out your experience of Malta. The easiest way to do this is to take a Malta Panorama coach tour. The itinerary can vary, but typically begins at one of Malta's most remarkable churches at Mosta, travels back in time to the island's original capital at Mdina, visits the Ta'Qali crafts village for a bit of shopping, stops for lunch at a village restaurant and ends at the picture-postcard fishing village of Marsaxlokk. If you hire a car, there are also temples and gardens to explore.

THINGS TO SEE & DO
Marsaxlokk ★★★
The name Marsaxlokk (pronounced 'Marsa-shlock') derives from *marsa* (the port) and *xlokk* (the sirocco wind). This is the most picturesque fishing village in Malta and, despite the coach-loads of visitors it receives daily, it has remained remarkably unspoiled. Its quayside is the perfect place for a cheap fish lunch and there is a daily market where you can haggle over lace tablecloths and other goods.

Mdina ★★★
The Silent City of Mdina (pronounced 'Im-deena') is a highlight of any Malta tour. Malta Panorama tours usually visit the Mdina Dungeon, the Mdina Experience and Medieval Times (see page 60).

Mosta Dome (The Church of St Mary) ★
This church was built between 1833 and 1860. Its portico and triangular gable are based on the Pantheon in Rome, but more famous is its dome, which measures 40 m (122 ft) in internal diameter and has given it its more familiar name. This is claimed to be the third-largest church dome in the world after St Peter's, in Rome and St Sophia, in Istanbul.

● *Marsaxlokk*

EYE-TO-EYE CONTACT
Few visitors leave Marsaxlokk without taking a picture of the traditional Maltese fishing boat, the *luzzu* (pronounced 'lut-sue'). Each *luzzu* is painted on either side of its unusually high prow with its own pair of eyes. This tradition goes back, along with the design of the *luzzu*, to Phoenician times (some 2500 years ago) when the eye was first painted as a good-luck charm to ward off the dreaded Evil Eye. Ironically, often painted alongside this pagan charm is the name of a Catholic saint.

It is said that the dome was not built so large as an act of deliberate pomposity, but because the church was literally built around an existing church, which could not be demolished until the new one was complete! The interior, lavishly decorated by local artists and trimmed with 18-carat gold leaf, is a marvellous sight.

During the Blitz of 1942 it is said that at least two bombs bounced off the dome. A third bomb, however, dropped straight through, while the church was full with some 300 parishioners. By good fortune, bad technology, or – as the Maltese say – by the grace of God, it failed to explode, and so another island miracle was born. A replica of the bomb is displayed in a side room of the church.

Palazzo Parisio ★

This 19th-century mansion, with the most ornate ballroom on the islands, has lavishly decorated ceilings and frescoes, antiques, paintings and bronzes. Its gardens originally stretched for half a mile and today, although smaller, are still impressive. ❸ Victory Square, Naxxar ❶ 21 412 461 ❶ Admission charge

San Anton Palace and Gardens ★★

Built by the Grand Master Antoine de Paule, San Anton Palace at Attard is now the Presidential Palace and is not open to the public. You can,

⚫ *Maltese fishing boat*

however, visit the splendid gardens, laid out in the 17th century, which contain various sub-tropical trees, such as the banyan.
ⓐ 7 km (4.5 miles) south west of Valletta

Ta'Qali ★★

The former site of an old RAF base, Ta'Qali (pronounced 'Ta-ali') is now a crafts village where local artisans work in filigree silver and gold, embroidery, lace, wool, glass, metal and other traditional Maltese handicrafts (see page 102). At Mdina Glass, part of Ta'Qali but located further away from the crafts village, you can watch the workers producing the traditional Maltese glass. ⓘ 21 415 786 ⓛ Open Mon–Fri 08.00–16.30, Sat 08.00–12.30

The Tarxien Temples ★★★

Located in the midst of a suburb in the town of Tarxien, the Tarxien Temples (pronounced 'Tar-she-en') were built between 3800 and 2500 BC. Stonehenge is about the same age. This is Malta's largest temple complex, and three of its six temples have been partially reconstructed. The Central Temple is the most impressive and was the last to be built. There are many fascinating remains, including altars with animal reliefs, an enormous stone bowl used for ritual purposes, and stone balls thought to have been used to roll the huge stones of the temple into position. Nearby is Malta's most fascinating temple complex, the subterranean Hypogeum. ⓐ Tarxien Temples and Hypogeum ⓛ Open 07.45–14.00 (16 June–30 Sept); Mon–Sat 08.30–16.30, Sun until 15.00 (1 Oct–15 June)

◆ The Blue Lagoon and view of Comino

Mediterranean cruise

Located far from the polluting influence of mainland Europe, the blue waters around Malta are some of the clearest and cleanest in the Mediterranean. You cannot say you have truly seen the Maltese archipelago unless you have explored its coastline from the seaboard side at least once. Here is a taste of the tours on offer – check with the tourist office for further details.

THINGS TO SEE & DO

The Blue Lagoon ★★★

Not to be confused with the Blue Grotto (see page 88), the glorious waters that divide the island of Comino from the islet of Cominotto are the biggest draw in Maltese cruising. Shallow and sheltered, the waters are not only a lovely inviting colour but they are warm as well. Some trips make this their only destination for the whole day – great if you just want to laze around but with little to offer in the way of coastal sightseeing. This idyllic place can become very crowded, which means your boat may anchor a little way out, leaving you a long swim before you can put your feet down – check before you book. The Blue Lagoon is also perfect for scuba diving and several diving schools run organized trips to here.

Grand Harbour tour ★★★

The defence system that protects Valletta and the Three Cities is unquestionably one of the world's greatest feats of military architecture. All the more remarkable is the fact that many of these bastions and fortifications were built over 400 years ago. The only way to appreciate this amazing complex is from the water, on a Grand Harbour Tour, with commentary full of lively anecdotes. ❸ Departs from Sliema ❶ Tours last 90 minutes

Helicopter tour ★★★

This is without doubt the most spectacular way of seeing the islands. Viewed from the air, Malta takes on a completely new dimension – often

cluttered and untidy at ground level, the island seems neat and well ordered from the air, especially the grid-pattern streets of Valletta. Other highlights include Grand Harbour, Mdina, Victoria (Gozo) and the Blue Lagoon. Trips take off from the international airport and, with just a 30-minute check-in, there is a minimum of fuss and delay.

 Helicopter trips last either 20 or 40 minutes. The former covers just Malta, the latter also goes to Gozo. Time in the air quite literally flies by, so the longer trip is recommended if you can afford it.

Do the Oki-Koki ★★

The Oki-Koki speedboats of the Blue Lagoon are great fun, due in no small part to the irrepressible characters who pilot them. They will collect you from your boat, take you on a short but very high-speed thrill ride, then slow down to a sea-snail's pace as you explore the caves. These compare favourably with Malta's famous Blue Grotto (see page 88).

The 'Round Malta' cruise ★★★

Departing from Sliema, this tour takes you clockwise around the island, to the picturesque fishing village of Marsaxlokk (see page 80), and the less-than-picturesque industrial Malta Freeport. The tour continues past the famous Blue Grotto (see page 88), dramatic Dingli Cliffs (see page 91), the sandy beaches of Golden Bay (see page 30) and the strange sight of Sweethaven Village (see page 34). A leisurely stop is made in the Blue Lagoon for a swim and the option of 'doing the Oki-Koki' (see above). Lunch is served on board, then it's anchors away, and off to Sliema via St Paul's Bay and the little islands where the Apostle was shipwrecked.

Sailing cruise ★

Most cruise boats are motorized. If you would prefer a more romantic voyage, try the *Fernandes* or the *Hera*, beautiful Turkish gulets (pronounced 'goo-let') or the fully rigged 70-year-old schooner, *Charlotte Louise*. Combining old-fashioned sail and sleek modernity is the *Spirit of Malta* (summer only), bringing a touch of the Caribbean to Malta, with

⬥ *Diving along the coast of Malta*

its lively music and unrationed rum. Most cruises return by 18.00, but when the sun goes down the fun begins on the 'Fernandes Sunday Sunset Cruise' and the 'Spirit of Malta Party Night'.

Underwater safari ★

If you would like to see what is going on beneath the waves, but you would rather not get your feet wet, or have to struggle into a wetsuit and snorkel, then the Underwater Safari is the cruise for you.

Tour boats operating out of Sliema and Bugibba have a specially designed observation keel below sea level, which seats 38 passengers and allows unimpaired views of some of the clearest and cleanest waters in the Mediterranean.

There are no tropical colours or coral reefs down here but a generous sprinkling of fish food ensures an abundant following and an expert marine biologist provides a commentary throughout the tour. On the Bugibba safari, you will also see two wrecks: *HMS Kingston* was sent to the bottom during World War II, whereas the *MV Hanini*, built in Scotland in 1924, was sunk deliberately as an artificial reef to attract fish.

The Blue Grotto & the south-west

The south-west coast of the island is well known for its rugged rocky scenery. The Blue Grotto is Malta's most famous natural formation but the cliffs of Dingli are the most spectacular. Between these lie the island's most dramatically sited temples.

THINGS TO SEE & DO

The Blue Grotto ★★★

The Blue Grotto is the biggest and best of a series of sea caves and archways near the village of Zurrieq (pronounced 'Zur-ree-ay'). Small boats pick up passengers in the sheltered picturesque rocky inlet of Wied-iz-Zurrieq and take them on a 25-minute tour. The eroded limestone grottoes and arches are awesome in scale, and the effect of sunlight on the water is magical. The water is brilliantly clear and in the caves it takes on a deep blue hue as the sunlight reflects off the caves and back into the water. Put your hand in the water and even it will look blue!

Buskett Gardens ★★

Most of Malta's trees were cut down a long time ago by medieval ship builders and Buskett Gardens is the only reminder today that this was once a wooded island. The term 'gardens' is, in fact, a bit of a misnomer, as most of this area consists simply of woodland. Not surprisingly, given its rarity value, it is a popular place for picnics, and on 29 June (the feast of St Peter and St Paul – also known as *Mnarja*, pronounced 'Im-nar-yah'), thousands of people come here to celebrate.

The attractions of the area have also long been appreciated by Maltese rulers. On the edge of Buskett Gardens is Verdala Palace, built in 1586 as a summer residence for the Grand Master of the Knights of St John. Today it is the summer house of the President of Malta.

◗ *The Blue Grotto*

◆ *Mnajdra*

Dingli Cliffs ★★

Malta's highest point is 250 m (830 ft) above sea-level, measured from the very edge of Dingli Cliffs down the sheer cliff face to the sea. Even on this sheer face, farmers have managed to cultivate some tiny terraces.

The Dingli Cliffs cover virtually the entire southern coast of Malta. The normal sightseeing route is to drive to Rabat and then on to the village of Dingli; the cliffs are a kilometre or so beyond the village.

Close to Dingli Cliffs is one of Malta's strangest mysteries. Cut into the flat rocky surface of the ground are long parallel grooves, rather like old tramlines. It is thought that these may have acted as runners for early carts, and are often referred to as cart ruts. The area near Dingli, where these are to be found in large numbers, is known as Clapham Junction.

Hagar Qim and Mnajdra ★

These two adjacent temple complexes are among the most impressive prehistoric monuments on Malta. Both are around 4500 to 5000 years old. The first site you will visit is Hagar Qim (pronounced 'Aa-jah eem'). Its name translates as 'standing stones', for very obvious reasons – one of its giant slabs alone measures 3 m by 7.5 m (9 ft by 23 ft). It is in better condition than its neighbour Mnajdra (pronounced 'Im-nah-ee-dra'), which was vandalized and seriously damaged a few years ago. Both were shrines to Mother Earth, and one school of thought was that the dead would only return to her womb if sacrifices were made at these places. Certainly offerings of animals' blood and milk were made at both temples.

Mnajdra looks on to the smallest of the Maltese islands, Filfla, a tiny rock which may have had a ritual importance once upon a time, though it was used by the British navy for target practice in more recent times. Today it is uninhabited and is protected as a bird reserve.

If you want a good place to cool off on this stretch of coast, you can't beat Ghar Lapsi, a superb natural lido, which is usually only frequented by locals. It is located around 6.5 km (4 miles) due west of Hagar Qim and Mnajdra.

◐ *Taormina and Mount Etna*

Sicily for the day

If you are the sort of person who likes to cram as many travel experiences as possible into a holiday, then it would be a shame to miss out on seeing the island of Sicily. A super-fast catamaran will whisk you from island to island in just 90 minutes, then a luxury air-conditioned double-decker coach will take you to marvel at Mount Etna and to stroll through the streets of Taormina, one of the most beautiful small towns in the Mediterranean.

Be prepared for a long day. The ferry leaves early and returns late and there are several hours of coach travel in between. You may also want to take some seasickness pills before departing.

THE ROAD NORTH

The catamaran docks on the south coast of Sicily, at Pozzallo. The immediate countryside is, like that on Malta, mostly barren and flat. Soon, however, you will pass over two of Europe's highest road bridges and look down to the town of Modica. The landscape begins to rise and fall, and becomes surprisingly lush.

THINGS TO SEE & DO

Mount Etna ★★★

Rising above the plain of Catania, to a height of over 3000 m (11,000 ft), Etna is the highest volcano in Europe, and its most active. Over 135 eruptions have been recorded, the worst being in 1669 when lava reached as far afield as Catania, some 32 km (20 miles) away. In 1928, the village of Mascali was devastated. The mountain has also spewed out lava in 1971, 1983, 1992 and in 2001, and as you ascend the slopes, you will see the legacy of this destruction, with houses wrecked and buried up to their rooftops in ash and debris. Tempting fate, the locals continue to inhabit its slopes, and, as a reward, harvest its rich bounty. Etna's fertile soil produces wonderful fruits, vegetables, the island's best wines and some excellent olive oil.

Until the eruption of 2001, the tour stopped at Sylvester Craters, created by the 1892 eruption. This is a spectacular landscape, with massive panoramic views down the slopes. Dotted below are smaller and older volcanic cones, many now cloaked in greenery. The higher the mountain the darker the colours – reds and purples, and greys and blacks. In winter, snow caps the volcano and it becomes a popular ski resort. The area around the volcano is now a protected national park.

Taormina ★★★

Sicily's premier resort, Taormina, would figure highly in any Mediterranean beauty contest, not least for its magnificent hilltop setting, best appreciated from its Teatro Greco. Originally built by the Greeks, then rebuilt by the Romans when the town enjoyed considerable status and prosperity, this must be one of the most spectacularly sited

ancient amphitheatres in the world. Views plunge down to the coastline in three directions, including to the aptly named Isola Bella and to the lovely beach resort of Giardini Naxos, the site of the very first Sicilian colony, founded by Greek settlers. On a clear spring day with snow-capped Etna in the background, the scene is truly breathtaking.

If you have time, visit the lovely town gardens, known as the Villa Communale, signposted near the Teatro Greco.

Most of central Taormina's sights lie on, or just off, its pedestrianized main street, the Corso Umberto. Many of its lovely old buildings have been turned into shops or restaurants, but nonetheless retain great charm. Start your visit at the corner of Piazza Emanuele and Corso Umberto, where you will find the Palazzo Corvaja, a 15th-century house which once housed the Sicilian parliament. The upper part has a good museum of art (free admission), while down below is the tourist office where you can get a free map. Continue along the whole length of Corso Umberto. There is much to admire, including the Torre dell'Orologio (Clock Tower), halfway along the street, and the Duomo (Cathedral), towards the end.

RESTAURANTS

There are restaurants and cafés at every turn in Taormina, though remember the Italian tradition that a drink or snack seated is more expensive than one standing at the bar. Also be aware that you will be paying quite a hefty premium just for the privilege of being in Taormina.

SHOPPING

After the comparatively small choice of tourist shops in Malta, Taormina is an Aladdin's Cave. From the shops by the Sylvester Craters, take home a tiny piece of Mount Etna in the shape of lava-fashioned jewellery, or a bottle of the local liqueur, *Fuoco del Etna* ('Fire of Etna') in a lava-stone bottle. In Taormina you will see medieval-style wooden puppets, a form of theatre that goes back to Norman times.

🔺 *Fish dishes are a speciality in Malta*

Food & drink

There are few establishments in the tourist resorts that serve exclusively Maltese cuisine. Many restaurants serve a handful of Maltese dishes but alongside these you will find Italian and other international dishes on the menu. Italian is the most common style of restaurant on the island.

FOR STARTERS

Every Mediterranean country has a fish soup and Malta is no exception; here it is called *alijotta*. The most common soup is *minestra*, made of a host of different vegetables, like Italian minestrone. If you are a pasta fan, try the Italian-inspired *ravjul* (ravioli filled with cheese). A very typical Maltese cheese dish is *gbejniet* (or *gbejna*), a pungent round of peppered ewe's-milk cheese, usually served with salad.

FISH DISHES

These will vary by season and availability within the restaurant but typical fish dishes to look out for are *acciola* (amberjack), *cerna* (grouper), *espadon*, *pixxispad* or *pesce espada* (all names for swordfish) and *lampuki* (dorado). The latter is a Maltese speciality, and is in season from September to November. It is often served in a pie (*torta tal-lampuki*) mixed with tomatoes, onions, olives, and various other vegetables. A much more robust-tasting speciality is swordfish Maltese style, smothered in a tasty sauce of tomatoes and capers. Another enjoyable local seafood dish is octopus, often served in a dark tomato sauce. Other unusual fish names you may come across are *dott* (stone bass) and *dentici* (sea bream).

RABBIT

The islanders' favourite meat dish is *fenek* (rabbit). This may be served *biz-zalza* (casseroled) or fried. Rabbit is the Maltese celebration dish and a traditional *fenkata* evening usually comprises a menu of spaghetti with rabbit sauce, followed by roast rabbit, then by nuts and figs. As a special treat it may be served as a pie (*torta tal-fenek*) with pork, peas, tomatoes and other ingredients. You will have to use your fingers to get the bones out of the rabbit, but the dish is tasty and justifies the effort.

MORE MEAT DISHES

Aside from rabbit, the other classic Maltese meat dish is *bragioli*, made from a flattened beef fillet, stuffed with bacon, breadcrumbs and hard-boiled eggs, rolled up and simmered in wine with onions. Less common on restaurant menus are Maltese sausages, which are of the familiar British link variety (as opposed to the continental slicing style). Often flavoured with lemon and herbs, these are delicious.

CHEESE AND PASTA

Two favourite national dishes which strongly reflect the Italian influence are *timpana* – baked macaroni with meat, eggs and cheese (and perhaps peas and aubergines), topped with flaky pastry – and *ross-fil-forn* – savoury rice, baked with eggs and meat. You may also find these sold from street stalls in square containers as takeaway snacks.

SNACKS

Typical Maltese snacks are sold in cafés or street kiosks. The ubiquitous lunchtime filler is *hobz biz zejt;* which translates as 'bread with oil'. This is a delicious, typically Mediterranean, snack of bread smeared with a paste of tomatoes, garlic, capers and olive oil, then filled with tuna, olives and salad. It may also be served toasted (like Italian bruschetta) as a starter in restaurants. Some places advertise *hobz biz zejt* as 'Maltese Bread'.

A favourite morning snack is a *pastizzi rikotta* (flaky ricotta-cheese envelope) or a *qassatat* (pronounced 'ass-er-tat'), a round flaky or shortcrust pie, filled either with cheese or yellow marrowfat peas. The latter is sometimes referred to as a *pizelli*. Both are sold fresh from the oven, and are best eaten warm.

⬥ Olive oil – a staple ingredient in Mediterranean cooking and the perfect
accompaniment to bread

SWEET THINGS

The Maltese have a sweet tooth and it is always a treat to pop into a
pastizzerija for a coffee, pastry or other confections on offer. Nougat is
very popular and nougat vendors are an integral part of the village *festa*.

DRINKS

The Maltese have inherited coffee from the Italians and tea from the
British, but coffee is nearly always a better bet. The British have also
bequeathed to the Maltese a dark, cold, fizzy, pale ale, sold almost
everywhere under the Hopleaf brand. Cisk Lager (pronounced 'Chisk')
is its companion brew. Another beer-based drink, with which older
holidaymakers will be familiar, is Farson's Shandy. Maltese wines have
come on in leaps and bounds in recent years and good quality wines by
Marsovin, the local standard bearer, are excellent. Gozo makes its own
wines, which are gutsy and with a higher than average alcoholic content.
The national soft drink is Kinnie, a refreshing cola-style beverage,
flavoured with bitter oranges and aromatic herbs.

Menu decoder

Most restaurants in Malta serve international food, but you may come across the following Maltese specialities in baker's shops, street stalls or rural cafes.

alijotta Fish soup, powerfully packed with garlic.

kabocci mimlija Cabbage leaves stuffed with minced beef or cheese.

kanolli ta-rrikotta Croissants stuffed with ricotta cheese blended with chocolate, almonds and preserved cherries.

kappunata Similar to ratatouille, a vegetable stew made with aubergines, peppers, onions tomatoes and courgettes, flavoured with garlic and capers.

kinnie A bitter but refreshing local drink made from oranges and wormwood (a type of herb).

pastizzi Puff-pastry pasties stuffed with mashed peas and spices or ricotta cheese.

ravjul Ravioli with a difference – stuffed with locally made ricotta cheese.

timpana Another traditional pie, this time of Sicilian origin, made from minced beef, potatoes, eggs and pasta in a white sauce.

THE SMELL OF THE EAST
That tempting aroma that wafts around the main gate to Valletta comes from *mqarets*, deep-fried date pastries, which are part of the island's Arab legacy.

◆ *Open-air dining, Valletta*

torta tal lampuki A traditional pie of Arabic origin (blending sweet and savoury ingredients) eaten as a summer snack; different cooks have different recipes combining *lampuki* (also known as dorado – a meaty white fish similar to mackerel) with some or all of the following: spinach, puréed cauliflower, onions, garlic, tomatoes, chestnuts and sultanas.

LIFESTYLE

Shopping

CRAFTS VILLAGES

For the best range of Maltese handicrafts – lace, filigree jewellery, chunky woollen jumpers, woodwork, metalwork, glass, and so on – try the **Ta'Qali crafts village**, on Malta, or the smaller complex of **Ta'Dbiegi**, just outside San Lawrenz, on Gozo (see page 66).

GLASSWARE

Glass is the island's most striking product, often produced in beautiful hues of gold and brown or blue. Maltese and Gozitan blown glass is not cheap, but the quality is high and you can watch the pieces being made.

LACE

Lace is the island speciality. Look out for tablecloths, napkins, shawls and handkerchiefs. Lacemakers are literally a dying breed on the islands, and if you are not buying from a traditional outlet, where you can see artisans at work, you should beware of imitations imported from the Far East.

MARKETS

The markets in Valletta are the best on the island. The Sunday morning market, known as the Monti, just outside the City Gate, has an interesting flea-market section but is mostly full of tourist fare and counterfeit products from the Far East. There is a lively bustle to the market, and it is worth a visit to see a slice of everyday Maltese life. The daily market on Triq Mercanti/Merchants' Street features much the same style of merchandise. Pop into the indoor market on the same street to catch the colourful fruit and vegetable stands and delicatessens.

SILVER & GOLD

More portable than glass, and often just as beautiful, is the delicate filigree silver and gold jewellery produced by Maltese artisans. You can see them at work in many places and prices are often keen.

🔺 *Traditional lace weaver*

VALLETTA

Valletta is not so much for shoppers as shop lovers. Here you will still find small specialist shops with beautiful facades that have survived, virtually untouched, since the 1940s. This is the place to buy silver filigree jewellery, Maltese stamps, glassware and other island specialities from enthusiastic shop owners who know their business inside out.

> ↘ If you're buying for children, note that Playmobil® is made on the island and sells for around half the price paid in the UK. Bags of seconds can be bought very cheaply at Valletta's Sunday market.

WINTER WOOLLIES

If the weather turns cold, or the wind blows hard, you'll appreciate the islands' woollens, particularly the chunky Aran-style knitted jumpers that are a speciality of Gozo. Prices are very reasonable.

Kids

ANIMAL WORLD & THE LSW RAILWAY PARK

Recent additions to the scene, and sure to be popular with younger kids include **Animal World** – a mini zoo that showcases monkeys, llamas, mountain goats, maras and reindeers – and the **Railway Park**, which consists of a miniature passenger carrying train with 244 m (800 ft) of track winding through gardens and the animal park. ❷ Razzett tal-Hbiberija, Marsascala ❶ 21 636 526 ❶ Admission charge

HORSE RIDING

If they are old enough to hold on then they are probably old enough to ride a horse at the Golden Bay stables (see page 29). The owners are very friendly, are accustomed to dealing with children, and use special safety harnesses to prevent accidents.

WHITE ROCKS

White Rocks is 9.5 km (6 miles) north of Valletta on the coast road to St Paul's Bay and is home to three family attractions. The **Splash 'n' Fun Water Park** (🕒 Open daily, summer only) is an attractive small lido with a large area of water-slides and tubes. Adjacent is the **Mediterraneo Marine Park**, small but professionally run, with sea lions, pelicans and a small aquarium area but the stars are undoubtedly the park's dolphins, rescued from the Black Sea, who perform all the usual crowd-pleasing stunts. For little ones there is also a playground area with a bright and lively dinosaur theme. ❶ 21 372 218 🕒 Open April–Sept – shows: sea lions 10.45 and 14.30,;dolphins 11.30 and 15.30 ❶ Admission charge

YOUNG TEENAGERS

Pack your children off to one of the special, alcohol-free, early evening weekend discos in Paceville (at St Julian's), or make a family visit to the ten-pin bowling alleys at **Eden Super Bowl**, at St George's Bay. If the thought of Mdina, the Silent City, doesn't appeal, tell them about **Mdina Dungeon** – gruesome waxworks of actual medieval horrors (see page 60).

● *Malta offers lots of opportunities for children to play in the water*

Keep an eye open in summer for fly-posters advertising local events, including the top-quality Italian circuses that occasionally visit the island.

⬧ *You may come across a house such as this on a walk around Gozo*

Sports & activities

HORSE RIDING

The friendly, helpful Golden Bay riding centre is equally at home with experienced riders and complete novices. You can ride for one or two hours, following trails along the coastal paths and overlooking the beaches, among some of the island's least-spoiled countryside.
📞 21 573 360 ❶ Book ahead

MARSA SPORTS CENTRE

Right in the centre of the island, the Marsa Sports complex offers a wide range of activities. This includes the only golf course on Malta – the 18-hole Royal Malta Club (equipment is for hire) – 17 tennis courts, five squash courts, mini-golf, an open-air swimming pool and billiards.

TYPICALLY MALTESE

Horse racing, of the trotting variety, is the most popular spectator sport in Malta. Jockeys do not ride the horses but are pulled along behind on a flimsy-looking trap. The track is at Marsa (public buses and organized excursions run there) and meetings on winter Sundays pull in large crowds. Racing continues throughout most of the year. You can enjoy a flutter on the tote or with the course bookies. The other Maltese sporting speciality is water-polo. You can see top-quality league games staged in the 'pitches' on the seafront at several places including Sliema, St Paul's Bay, and St Julian's, on summer weekends 🕒 See local papers for details of fixtures

WALKING

March to June, and October are the best months for walking in Malta and Gozo. The latter is particularly pleasant as there is more unspoiled countryside to ramble. Ask at the tourist office for a local guide to take you out or alternatively do it yourself with the assistance of *Hiking in Malta, Gozo & Comino*, published by J. Kolb Publishing (mostly aimed at experienced walkers), available at bookshops in Valletta, if not in your resort.

WATER SPORTS

The island's clear blue waters and warm summer seas (averaging 23°C/73.5°F) mean that diving is a very popular pastime. The scarcity of sand, lack of pollution and stillness of the virtually tide-free waters all contribute to excellent visibility, which on average is up to 30 m (100 ft). You won't see too many exotic fish, but there are caves and grottoes to explore, and good wreck diving. Most clubs on the island operate to a high standard, are PADI and BSAC affiliated, and are well equipped to deal with beginners and experienced divers.

At Golden Bay, Mellieha Bay, and at various lidos around the island, you will find the usual range of resort water sports, including windsurfing (the conditions at Mellieha are excellent), waterskiing and jet skis.

LIFESTYLE

Festivals & events

CARNIVAL

Held in the week before Lent (usually around late February) this is one of the most colourful events of the Maltese festival calendar. It culminates in a procession of floats featuring grotesque characters with giant heads. Open-air dancing competitions are also held. Festivities take place in various locations, though the main ones are in Valletta and just outside, at Floriana.

FESTA

The island's most visual cultural celebration is the village *festa*, or festival. The purpose of the *festa* is to honour the village patron saint. Various events, mostly of a religious nature, are conducted from Wednesday through to Sunday. The religious highlight is the Sunday night procession, when a weighty statue of the saint is carried shoulder high by sturdy villagers.

The whole village will be festooned with banners, and the centrepiece is the church, gloriously decorated with hundreds of coloured lights outside and with sumptuous red damask inside. Other buildings, such as the village band club, will also be lavishly decorated.

The village brass band, and possibly visiting brass bands, parade and play, and, on Saturday night, singers may join in to perform an outdoor concert in the village square.

Traditional Maltese nougat is sold from gleaming, portable wood-and-glass cabinets, and there are fast-food vendors too. Saturday night climaxes with a marvellous display of powerful set-piece fireworks on large wooden stands dotted around the village centre. Aerial fireworks are saved until the sun sets and bring the *festa* to a spectacular finale.

The *festa* season begins in mid-April and lasts until September, with at least one festival taking place somewhere each week.

⬥ *Festa night*

● *Religious procession*

Large crowds pack the village square on the Saturday night of a *festa*, so choose your place carefully for the fireworks (which usually start around 23.00). You want to be close enough to see them but not so close that they are dangerous or so you are knocked over in the rush to get out of the way.

THE PERFORMING ARTS

For an evening of conventional high culture, visit Valletta's Manoel Theatre. This little gem stages regular productions of ballet, opera, concerts and plays. Look in the local paper to see what is on. A free lunchtime concert is held in one of the theatre's recital rooms every Wednesday.

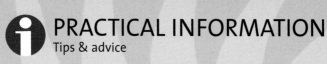

Preparing to go

GETTING THERE

The cheapest way to get to Malta is to book a package holiday with one of the leading tour operators. You should also check the Travel supplements of the weekend newspapers, such as the *Sunday Telegraph*, and *The Sunday Times*. They often carry adverts for inexpensive flights, as well as classified adverts for privately owned villas and apartments to rent in most popular holiday destinations.

If your travelling times are flexible, and if you can avoid the school holidays, you can also find some very cheap last-minute deals using the websites of the leading holiday companies.

BEFORE YOU LEAVE

Holidays should be about fun and relaxation, so avoid last-minute panics and stress by making your preparations well in advance.

MALTA TOURIST OFFICE

Further information about Malta can be obtained from the ❸ Malta Tourist Office, Unit C Parkhouse, 14 Northfields, London SW18 1DD
❶ 020 8877 6990 ❶ 020 8874 9416 Ⓦ www.visitmalta.com

It is not necessary to have inoculations to travel in Europe, but you should make sure you and your family are up to date with the basics, such as tetanus. It is a good idea to pack a small first-aid kit to carry with you containing plasters, antiseptic cream, travel sickness pills, insect repellent and/or bite relief cream, antihistamine tablets, upset stomach remedies and painkillers. Sun lotion can be more expensive in Malta than in the UK so it is worth taking a good selection especially of the higher factor lotions if you have children with you, and don't forget after-sun cream as well. If you are taking prescription medicines, ensure that you take enough for the duration of your visit – you may find it impossible to obtain the same medicines in Malta. It is also worth having a dental check-up before you go.

DOCUMENTS

The most important documents you will need are your tickets and your passport. Check well in advance that your passport is up to date and has at least three months left to run (six months is even better). All children, including newborn babies, need their own passport now, unless they are already included on the passport of the person they are travelling with. It generally takes at least three weeks to process a passport renewal. This can be longer in the run-up to the summer months. For the latest information on how to renew your passport and the processing times call the **Passport Agency** on ☎ 0870 521 0410 or ⓦ www.ukpa.gov.uk

You should check the details of your travel tickets well before your departure, ensuring that the timings and dates are correct.

If you are thinking of hiring a car while you are away, you will need to have your driving licence with you. If you want more than one driver for the car, the other drivers must have their licence too.

MONEY

You will need some currency before you go, especially if your flight gets you to your destination at the weekend or late in the day after the banks have closed. Traveller's cheques are the safest way to carry money because the money will be refunded if the cheques are lost or stolen. To buy traveller's cheques or exchange money at a bank you may need to give up to a week's notice, depending on the quantity of foreign currency you require.

You can exchange money at the airport before you depart. You should also make sure that your credit, charge and debit cards are up to date – you do not want them to expire mid holiday – and that your credit limit is sufficient to allow you to make those holiday purchases. Don't forget, too, to check your PIN numbers in case you haven't used them for a while – you may want to draw money from cash dispensers while you are away. Ring your bank or card company and they will help you out.

INSURANCE

Have you got sufficient cover for your holiday? Check that your policy covers you adequately for loss of possessions and valuables, for activities you might want to try – such as scuba-diving, horse-riding, or water sports – and for emergency medical and dental treatment, including flights home if required.

From January 2006, the European Helath Insurance Card (EHIC) replaces the old E111 form, which enables you to reclaim the costs of some medical treatment incurred while travelling in EU countries for citizens of EU countries. For information and an application form, enquire at the post office or visit Ⓦ www.dh.gov.u/travellers

CLIMATE

Malta's climate is typically Mediterranean with hot, dry summers, warm and infrequently wet autumns, and short, cool winters. The temperature is stable with monthly averages ranging from 12°C (54°F) to 31°C (88°F).

PETS

Remember to make arrangements for the care of your pets while you are away – book them into a reputable cat or dog hotel, or make arrangements with a trustworthy neighbour to ensure that they are properly fed, watered and exercised while you are on holiday.

SECURITY

- Cancel milk, newspapers and other regular deliveries so that post and milk does not pile up on the doorstep, indicating that you are away.
- Let the postman know where to leave parcels and bulky mail that will not go through your letterbox – ideally with a next-door neighbour.

TELEPHONING MALTA

To call Malta from the UK, dial 00 356 then the nine-digit number – there's no need to wait for a dialling tone.

- If possible, arrange for a friend or neighbour to visit regularly, closing and opening curtains in the evening and morning, and switching lights on and off to give the impression that the house is being lived in.
- Consider buying electrical timing devices that will switch lights and radios on and off, again to give the impression that there is someone in the house.
- Let Neighbourhood Watch representativesknow that you will be away so that they can keep an eye on your home.
- If you have a burglar alarm, make sure that it is serviced and working properly and is switched on when you leave (you may find that your insurance policy requires this). Ensure that a neighbour is able to gain access to the alarm to turn it off if it is set off accidentally.
- If you are leaving cars unattended, put them in a garage, if possible, and leave a key with a neighbour in case the alarm goes off.

AIRPORT PARKING & ACCOMMODATION

If you intend to leave your car in an airport car park while you are away, or stay the night at an airport hotel before or after your flight, you should book well ahead to take advantage of hotel discounts or cheap off-airport parking. Airport accommodation gets booked up several weeks in advance, especially during the height of the holiday season. Check whether the hotel offers free parking for the duration of the holiday – often the savings made on parking costs can significantly reduce the accommodation price.

PACKING TIPS

Baggage allowances vary according to the airline, destination and the class of travel, but 20 kg (44 lb) per person is the norm for luggage that is carried in the hold (it usually tells you what the weight limit is on your ticket). You are also allowed one item of cabin baggage weighing no more than 5kg (11lb), and measuring 46 by 30 by 23 cm (18 by 12 by 9 inches).

In addition, you can usually carry your airport purchases, umbrella, handbag, coat, camera, as hand baggage. Large items – surfboards, golf-clubs, collapsible wheelchairs and pushchairs – are usually charged as extras – let the airline know in advance that you want to bring these.

CHECK-IN, PASSPORT CONTROL & CUSTOMS

First-time travellers can often find airport security intimidating, but it is all very easy really.

- Check-in desks usually open two or three hours before the flight is due to depart. Arrive early for the best choice of seats.
- Look for your flight number on the TV monitors in the check-in area, and find the relevant check-in desk. Your tickets will be checked and your luggage taken. Take your boarding card and go to the departure gate. Here your hand luggage will be X-rayed and your passport checked.
- In the departure area, you can shop and relax, but watch the monitors that tell you when to board – usually about 30 minutes before take-off. Go to the departure gate shown on the monitor and follow the instructions given to you by the airline staff.

Entry or transit visas are not required – for stays of up to three months for holidays or unpaid business trips – by nationals of most Commonwealth countries, UK dependencies or Council of Europe members. Council of Europe nationals may enter Malta with a national identity card.

If a stay of longer than three months is planned, applications should be made in person, before the end of the initial three months period, to the Principal Immigration Officer, Immigration Police, Police Headquarters, Floriana.

Nationals of countries that require a visa should obtain these from a Maltese embassy or consulate. Where neither of these is available a written request should be made to the Commissioner of Police, Police Headquarters, Floriana – faxed applications are acceptable ☎ 21 247 777 Application forms can also be downloaded from ⓦ www.foreign.gov.mt

Visitors requiring an entry visa to Malta and who undertake day trips (of less than 24 hours) to another country are exempted from paying another entry visa on their return to Malta.

During your stay

AIRPORTS

Malta International Airport is located next to the village of Gudja, 10 km (6 miles) from Valletta.

Landside facilities at MIA include airline ticketing offices and aviation counter, baby-care rooms, two banks, cafeterias, car hire offices, chapel, drugstore, flight information counter, florist, international telephone, lotto booth, newsagent, post office, restaurant, sweets shop, telecommunications centre, tourist information counter and a viewing gallery.

Air-side facilities include baby-care facilities, bar/cafeteria, duty free shops – in both arrivals and departure halls – and three VIP/executive lounges (the Ewropa Lounge is operated by Air Malta whilst the La Valette Executive and Gerolamo Cassar (arrivals hall) lounges are run by the airport operating company – Malta International Airport plc).

BEACHES

There are no lifeguards at public beaches or life-saving amenities available, consequently care must be taken to avoid mishaps. Bear in mind that the strong winds that develop in the hotter months can quickly change a safe beach into a not-so-safe one, and some can have strong currents the further out you go.

The Maltese islands are not renowned for their sandy beaches, however there are several in the north of Malta; the best are Mellieha Bay, Gnejna Bay, Golden Bay, Ghajn Tuffieha and Paradise Bay. In the south, the finest is Pretty Bay in Birzebbugia.

> **BEACH SAFETY**
> A flag system operates, to advise you of swimming conditions.
> **Red** = dangerous – no swimming at all
> **Green** = safe bathing conditions for all
> **Yellow** = strong swimmers only – apply caution

Comino has two sandy beaches: Sta Marija Bay and St Niklaw Bay. In Gozo Ramla Bay stands out for its beautiful red sand. Rock bathing is possible at almost all other beach sites. On some beaches you can rent self-drive speed boats, canoes, surf-boards, waterskis, jet skis and go paragliding.

CASINOS

There are three casinos in Malta: the Dragonara Casino in St Julian's, the Casinò di Venezia in Vittoriosa and the Oracle Casino at the New Dolmen Hotel in Qawra. You need an identity card or passport for admittance. Foreign nationals must be 18, and Maltese citizens 25, to enter.

CURRENCY

The unit of currency is the Malta Lira, abbreviated as 'Lm' and divided into 100 cents (c); each cent is nominally divided into 10 mils (m).
Coins 1c, 2c, 5c, 10c, 25c, 50c, Lm1.
Notes Lm2, Lm5, Lm10, Lm20.

Currency exchange Cash and traveller's cheques can be exchanged at banks, foreign exchange bureaux, most hotels, restaurants and at larger shops. The exchange slip is required to change local currency back to foreign denominations on departure. Exchange rates offered by hotels, restaurants and especially shops are far inferior to those available at banks.

Currency regulations and restrictions There is no limit on the amount of foreign currency imported by individuals into Malta, if it is declared on arrival. The maximum amount of Maltese currency that may be brought into the country is Lm1000 per person. Visitors may export the foreign currency brought to Malta up to the amount declared on arrival. However, no more than Lm1000 in Maltese currency may be exported.

On leaving Malta, have your copy of the foreign exchange sales ticket issued by a bank or forex bureau – customs authorities have the power to search you and question you on the sum of money you carry. Maltese currency is best converted back into sterling at UK airport banks.

ELECTRICITY

The electrical supply is 240 volts, single phase, 50 cycles. The 13 amps, British-style three-pin rectangular sockets are used in Malta. If you are considering buying electrical appliances to take home, always check that they will work in the UK before you buy.

FACILITIES FOR VISITORS WITH DISABILITIES

The upmarket hotels offer facilities for those with disabilities, and many of them have rooms specifically catering for the physically challenged. Unfortunately, the same cannot be said for the rest of the country.

GETTING AROUND

Driving As in many Commonwealth countries, driving in Malta is on the left. There is a speed limit of 80 km/h (50 mph) on highways and 50 km/h (30 mph) in urban areas. Third-party insurance is advisable, as the islands' accident rate is one of the highest in Europe. International and national driving licences are acceptable and may be endorsed free to visitors at police headquarters in Floriana 🛈 21 224001/9

In the event of an accident, telephone the police on 191 and, if required, an ambulance, on 196. If the collision is severe, drivers should not move cars until the police have arrived and taken note of the incident. Insurance companies will not entertain any claim unless it is supported by a police report. In the event of minor accidents a police report is not necessary, but a form – obtained from any police station – must be completed.

Bus Hop aboard one of the many old British-style buses (painted yellow) that make up the island's public transport fleet. Just a few cents will take you all the way to the other side of the island (it isn't obligatory, but to avoid delays, try to have the right change to hand). Most routes have a flat fare, irrespective of how far you travel. Most also start and end in Valletta, where you have to change to continue your journey. In summer, however, special routes are put on for visitors, typically going from the resorts to the main beaches and other attractions.

Taxi These are generally painted white, and can be hailed in the street or from your hotel. Fares are usually a matter for prior agreement, as the meter is often conveniently 'not working' or switched off. Prices increase sharply after midnight so, if you want a night out, it is a good idea to ask your hotel to book a taxi and agree the fare in advance.

HEALTH MATTERS

Health hazards Standards are high and the only real hazard is sunburn. The water is generally safe to drink though it is not very palatable. Malta offers free healthcare to British nationals. There are English-speaking doctors and clinics in each resort.

Malta has reciprocal health agreements with Australia and the United Kingdom. Nationals of these countries, visiting the islands for no longer than a month, are entitled to free medical and hospital care in both Gozo and Malta. Persons undergoing medical treatment – and who may need to bring medicines to Malta, or buy fresh supplies locally – are advised to obtain a letter of introduction from their GP. Most European prescriptions are available on the islands.

There are chemists throughout the islands – these are open during normal shopping hours. On Sundays, chemists open on a roster basis 09.00–12.30 in Malta and 07.30–11.00 in Gozo – check Sunday newspapers to see which ones are open.

There is one general hospital in Malta, St Luke's in Guardamangia, and one in Gozo, Gozo General Hospital in Victoria. There are also government health centres in several towns and villages, these open Mon–Fri 08.00–17.00 and Sat and Sun 08.00–13.00. The centres are open 24 hours a day for emergencies only.

MALTESE

The island's official languages are Maltese (Malti) and English, which almost everyone on the main island speaks. Normally it is only in the rural areas of Gozo where you may have difficulty in being understood. Nobody expects tourists to be good at Malti, which is an ancient language with very distinctive and unique sounds, but it is always nice to be able to say a few words in the local language. Here are some everyday phrases to try.

THE LANGUAGE

ENGLISH	MALTESE (pronunciation)
General vocabulary	
yes	*iva* (eeva)
no	*le* (lay)
please	*jekk joghghok* (yek keeoshbok)
thank you (very much)	*grazzi* (gratis)
You're welcome	*m'hemmx imnex* (mhemmsh imnesh)
Hello	*bongu* (bonjou)
goodbye	*sahha* (sah'ha)
good day	*il gurnata tajba* (eel journata taiba)
good night	*illej it tajjeb* (eel-lay it tie-eb)
excuse me	*scuzani* (scoozanee)
Help!	*ghajnuna* (aye-nuna)
today	*illum* (eel-oom)
tomorrow	*ghada* (ada)
yesterday	*ilbierah* (eel-beera)

Useful words and phrases

open	*iftah* (if-tah)
closed	*ghalaq* (ala)
push	*imbottar* (im-bottar)
pull	*igbet* (eeg-bet)
How much is it?	*kemm* (kemm)
expensive	*ghali* (ali)
bank	*ilbank*
bureau de change	*biex insarraf* (bish insarraf)
post office	*posta* (pos'ta)
duty chemist	*spizerija* (spizeria)
bank card	*bank card*

ENGLISH	**MALTESE** (pronunciation)
General vocabulary	
credit card	*credit card*
traveller's cheques	*traveller's cheques*
table	*mejda* (maida)
menu	*menu*
waiter	*waiter*
water	*ilma* (eelma)
fizzy/still water	*fizzi ilma* (fizzy eelma)
I don't understand	*mux qet mifmek* (moosh et mifmek)
The bill, please	*il cont*
Do you speak English?	*titkellem bli ingliz?* (titkellem blee ingliz)
My name is...	*jisimni...* (yi-simni)
Where are the toilets?	*fejn it toilets?* (fein it toilets?)
Where is there a telephone	*fejn hemm telephone?* (fein em telephone)
Can you call me a taxi?	*tista tajghatli taxi?* (tista tie-atle taxi?)

MEDIA

There are two locally published English language dailies – the *Malta Independent* and *The Times*. On Sundays, the *Malta Independent on Sunday*, *The Sunday Times* and *Malta Today* are available. The major English newspapers are also available from newsagents, these are normally available late in the afternoon.

OPENING HOURS

Banks These are generally open Mon–Fri 08.30–12.30 and until noon on Saturday. Many major banks have money-changing desks that are

TELEPHONING ABROAD

To call an overseas number from Malta, dial **oo** followed by the country code (UK = **44**), then the area code (minus the initial o) and then the number you want.

open in the afternoon, and there are lots of ATM facilities in the tourist centres. Exchange bureaux do not usually offer such good rates.

Chemists and shops Traditional shop opening hours (including chemists) are Mon–Sat 09.00–13.00 and 16.00–19.00. Many shops in resorts open throughout the day and also on Sunday.

Post Offices Standard post office opening hours are Mon–Fri 07.45–13.30, and 09.00–noon on Saturday (see also below).

Bars, cafés and restaurants Officially, alcohol may only be bought up to 01.00. Restaurants are not open before 11.30 and are closed between 15.00 and 19.00.

POST OFFICES

Malta has an efficient postal service. Most towns and villages have a post or sub-post office. Stamps are sold in post offices and hotels.
Malta Post Office ⓐ 305 Qormi Road, Qormi 🕒 Open Mon–Sat 07.45–18.30 (Oct–mid-June); Mon–Sat 07.30 to 18.00 (mid-June–30 Sept).
Gozo Post Office ⓐ 129 Republic Street, Victoria 🕒 Same as Malta, above

RELIGION

The majority of Maltese are Roman Catholic. There are small Anglican, Church of Scotland, Greek Catholic and Orthodox, Jewish and Muslim communities.

TELEPHONES

Local and international telephone calls can be made from hotel rooms, and credit cards are normally accepted. Fax machines are also available at most hotels. Most coin-operated public telephone boxes can only be used for local calls. For overseas calls, your best option is to buy a phonecard (from newsagents, Maltacom and souvenir shops).

Maltacom provides an international telephone and fax service in South Street, Valletta – only available Mon–Sat 07.30–18.30.

WHAT TO DO IN AN EMERGENCY
Staff manning the emergency services all speak perfect English.
On Malta Police ☎ 191; Ambulance ☎ 196; Fire ☎ 199.
On Gozo Police and fire ☎ 21 562 044; Ambulance ☎ 21 560 600.

Many of the larger towns and tourist resorts have a Maltacom office providing international calls and fax services. Many hotels now offer email facilities. There are also Internet cafés where one can send and receive email. Email-enabled phone booths have also been installed in the principal tourist resorts and larger towns.

TIME DIFFERENCES

Malta is on Central European Time (CET), one hour ahead of Greenwich Mean Time (GMT) in winter and two hours from the last Sunday in March until the last Sunday in October.

Malta is one of Europe's safest destinations. The main danger is theft of possessions from parked cars. Attendants will often look after your car at beaches and archaeological sites. It is customary to give them a small tip (around 10 to 25 cents).

WEIGHTS AND MEASURES

Imperial to metric
1 inch = 2.54 centimetres
1 foot = 30 centimetres
1 mile = 1.6 kilometres
1 ounce = 28 grams
1 pound = 454 grams
1 pint = 0.6 litres
1 gallon = 4.6 litres

Metric to imperial
1 centimetre = 0.4 inches
1 metre = 3 feet, 3 inches
1 kilometre = 0.6 miles
1 gram = 0.04 ounces
1 kilogram = 2.2 pounds
1 litre = 1.8 pints

 INDEX

INDEX

ACKNOWLEDGEMENTS

We would like to thank all the photographers, picture libraries and organisations for the loan of the photographs reproduced in this book, to whom copyright in the photograph belongs:
Donna Dailey (pages 28, 78);
Jupiter Images Corporation (page 125);
Malta Tourist Agency (pages 44, 90);
Pictures Colour Library Ltd (pages 37, 55, 92, 99);
Thomas Cook Tour Operations Ltd (pages 1, 5, 9, 13, 18–19, 22, 33, 41, 48, 57, 63, 68, 70, 77, 81, 83, 84, 87, 89, 95, 96, 101, 103, 105, 106, 109, 110).

We would also like to thank the following for their contribution to this series:
John Woodcock (map and symbols artwork);
Becky Alexander, Patricia Baker, Sophie Bevan, Judith Chamberlain-Webber, Nicky Gyopari, Stephanie Horner, Krystyna Mayer, Robin Pridy (editorial support);
Christine Engert, Suzie Johanson, Richard Lloyd, Richard Peters, Alistair Plumb, Jane Prior, Barbara Theisen, Ginny Zeal, Barbara Zuñiga (Design support).

Send your thoughts to
books@thomascook.com

- Found a beach bar, peaceful stretch of sand or must-see sight that we don't feature?

- Like to tip us off about any information that needs a little updating?

- Want to tell us what you love about this handy, little guidebook and more importantly how we can make it even handier?

Then here's your chance to tell all! Send us ideas, discoveries and recommendations today and then look out for your valuable input in the next edition of this title. And, as an extra 'thank you' from Thomas Cook Publishing, you'll be automatically entered into our exciting monthly prize draw.

Email to the above address or write to:
HotSpots Project Editor, Thomas Cook Publishing, PO Box 227, Unit 15/16, Coningsby Road, Peterborough PE3 8SB, UK.